GRAMMAR WORKBOO

EXERCISES
in ENGLISH

Teacher Guide

LEVEL E

LOYOLAPRESS.

CHICAGO

The Workout That Brings Mastery in Grammar, Usage, and Mechanics

Exercises in English is the perfect teaching tool for educators who want their students to be educationally fit and READY—ready to communicate effectively when writing or speaking, ready for everyday language arts tasks, ready for accelerated English-language learning, and ready for assessment. Here are some ways that a workout with Exercises in English helps students become READY for any language arts task that they encounter:

 RIGOROUS PRACTICE

Students are provided with a multitude of exercises on each page. With so many opportunities for learning, "practice makes perfect" is achievable!

 EXAMPLES AND DEFINITIONS

Success comes with systematic instruction. Each new grammar, usage, or mechanics concept is clearly explained through examples and definitions.

 ASSESSMENT

GUM scores increase as students are assessed and master their work with sentences, verbal agreement, and punctuation.

 DIAGRAMMING FOR IN-DEPTH LANGUAGE STUDY

When students diagram sentences, they create visual representations of their learning—they can actually see how words work together to make correctly constructed sentences.

 YEARLONG REINFORCEMENT FOR LEARNERS AT EVERY LEVEL

With six books of varying levels and a multitude of lessons in each book, students are provided with learning opportunities that last a full school year and beyond.

Inside Exercises in English

RIGOROUS PRACTICE

Focused skills are practiced in a variety of ways.

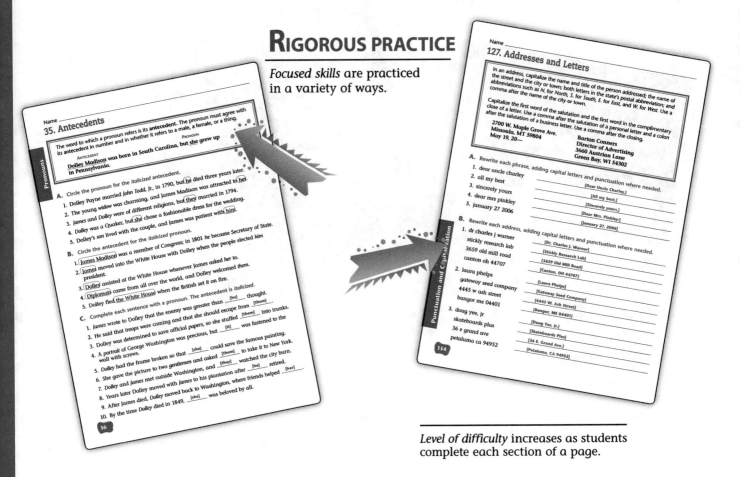

Name _____

35. Antecedents

The word to which a pronoun refers is its **antecedent**. The pronoun must agree with its antecedent in number and in whether it refers to a male, a female, or a thing.

ANTECEDENT   PRONOUN
Dolley Madison was born in South Carolina, but she grew up in Pennsylvania.

A. Circle the pronoun for the *italicized* antecedent.
1. *Dolley Payne* married John Todd, Jr., in 1790, but he died three years later.
2. The young *widow* was charming, and James Madison was attracted to her.
3. *James* and Dolley were of different religions, but they married in 1794.
4. *Dolley* was a Quaker, but she chose a fashionable dress for the wedding.
5. *Dolley's son* lived with the couple, and James was patient with him.

B. Circle the antecedent for the *italicized* pronoun.
1. James Madison was a member of Congress; in 1801 *he* became Secretary of State.
2. James moved into the White House with Dolley when the people elected *him* president.
3. Dolley assisted at the White House whenever James asked *her* to.
4. Diplomats came from all over the world, and Dolley welcomed *them*.
5. Dolley fled the White House when the British set *it* on fire.

C. Complete each sentence with a pronoun. The antecedent is *italicized*.
1. *James* wrote to Dolley that the enemy was greater than __[he]__ thought.
2. He said that *troops* were coming and that she should escape from __[them]__ into trunks.
3. Dolley was determined to save *official papers*, so she stuffed __[it]__ was fastened to the wall with screws.
4. A portrait of *George Washington* was precious, but __[she]__ could save the famous painting.
5. Dolley had the frame broken so that __[she]__ could take it to New York.
6. She gave the picture to two *gentlemen* and asked __[them]__ to watch the city burn.
7. Dolley and *James* met outside Washington, and __[they]__ watched the city burn.
8. Years later *Dolley* moved with James to his plantation after __[he]__ retired.
9. After James died, *Dolley* moved back to Washington, where friends helped __[her]__.
10. By the time *Dolley* died in 1849, __[she]__ was beloved by all.

36

Pronouns

Name _____

127. Addresses and Letters

In an address, capitalize the name and title of the person addressed; the name of the street and the city or town; both letters in the state's postal abbreviation; and abbreviations such as *N.* for *North, S.* for *South, E.* for *East,* and *W.* for *West.* Use a comma after the name of the city or town.

Capitalize the first word of the salutation and the first word in the complimentary close of a letter. Use a comma after the salutation of a personal letter and a colon after the salutation of a business letter. Use a comma after the closing.

2700 W. Maple Grove Ave.
Missoula, MT 59804
May 19, 20—

Barton Conners
Director of Advertising
3660 Austrian Lane
Green Bay, WI 54302

A. Rewrite each phrase, adding capital letters and punctuation where needed.
1. dear uncle charley   [Dear Uncle Charley.]
2. all my best   [All my best.]
3. sincerely yours   [Sincerely yours,]
4. dear mrs pinkley   [Dear Mrs. Pinkley.]
5. january 27 2006   [January 27, 2006]

B. Rewrite each address, adding capital letters and punctuation where needed.
1. dr charles j warner   [Dr. Charles J. Warner.]
   stickly research lab   [Stickly Research Lab]
   3659 old mill road   [3659 Old Mill Road]
   canton oh 44707   [Canton, OH 44707]
2. laura phelps   [Laura Phelps]
   gateway seed company   [Gateway Seed Company]
   4445 w ash street   [4445 W. Ash Street]
   bangor me 04401   [Bangor, ME 04401]
3. doug yee, jr   [Doug Yee, Jr.]
   skateboards plus   [Skateboards Plus]
   36 e grand ave   [36 E. Grand Ave.]
   petaluma ca 94952   [Petaluma, CA 94952]

134

Punctuation and Capitalization

Level of difficulty increases as students complete each section of a page.

EXAMPLES AND DEFINITIONS

Clear definitions and numerous examples guide instruction.

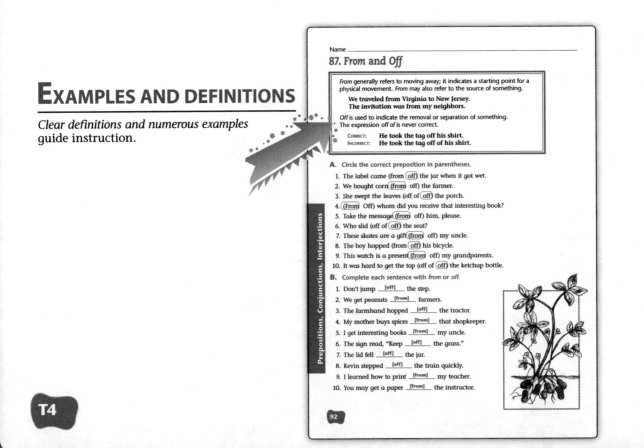

Name _____

87. From and Off

From generally refers to moving away; it indicates a starting point for a physical movement. *From* may also refer to the source of something.

    We traveled from Virginia to New Jersey.
    The invitation was from my neighbors.

Off is used to indicate the removal or separation of something. The expression *off of* is never correct.

CORRECT: **He took the tag off his shirt.**
INCORRECT: **He took the tag off of his shirt.**

A. Circle the correct preposition in parentheses.
1. The label came (from / **off**) the jar when it got wet.
2. We bought corn (**from** / off) the farmer.
3. She swept the leaves (off of / **off**) the porch.
4. (**From** / Off) whom did you receive that interesting book?
5. Take the message (**from** / off) him, please.
6. Who slid (off of / **off**) the seat?
7. These skates are a gift (**from** / off) my uncle.
8. The boy hopped (from / **off**) his bicycle.
9. This watch is a present (**from** / off) my grandparents.
10. It was hard to get the top (off of / **off**) the ketchup bottle.

B. Complete each sentence with *from* or *off*.
1. Don't jump __[off]__ the step.
2. We get peanuts __[from]__ farmers.
3. The farmhand hopped __[off]__ the tractor.
4. My mother buys spices __[from]__ that shopkeeper.
5. I get interesting books __[from]__ my uncle.
6. The sign read, "Keep __[off]__ the grass."
7. The lid fell __[off]__ the jar.
8. Kevin stepped __[off]__ the train quickly.
9. I learned how to print __[from]__ my teacher.
10. You may get a paper __[from]__ the instructor.

92

Prepositions, Conjunctions, Interjections

T4

ASSESSMENT

Comprehensive reviews allow for classroom assessment or preparation for standardized tests.

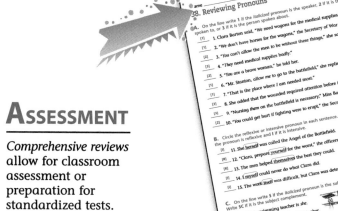

DIAGRAMMING FOR IN-DEPTH LANGUAGE STUDY

Sentence diagramming helps students better understand and remember concepts.

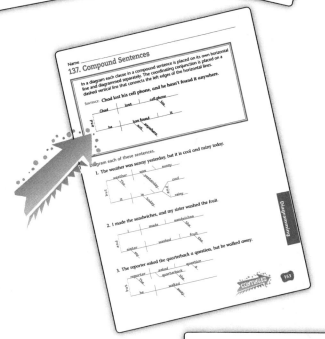

YEARLONG REINFORCEMENT FOR LEARNERS AT EVERY LEVEL

Leveled books allow for differentiated instruction. Determine which books to use based on individual student achievement rather than grade level.

Handbook of Terms invites all learners to refresh and expand their knowledge.

Handbook of Terms

ADJECTIVES

An **adjective** is a word that describes a noun or pronoun.

Articles point out nouns. *A*, *an*, and *the* are articles.

- *A* and *an* are the indefinite articles. An indefinite article refers to any of a class of things: *a banana*, *an elephant*. *The* is the definite article. The definite article refers to one or more specific things: *A pear* and *an apple* are in *the* blue bowl.

- When two or more nouns joined by *and* name different people, places, or things, use an article before each noun. When two or more nouns joined by *and* refer to the same person, place, or thing, use an article before the first noun only: *The singer* and *the dancer performed together. The actor and comedian is my cousin.*

Demonstrative adjectives point out specific persons, places, or things.

- *This* and *that* point out one person, place, or thing.
- *These* and *those* point out more than one person, place, or thing.
- *This* and *these* point out persons, places, or things that are near.
- *That* and *those* point out persons, places, or things that are farther away.

Descriptive adjectives tell about the size, shape, color, weight, or other qualities of the things they describe. A descriptive adjective can come before a noun: *sunny morning*, *hot day*. A descriptive adjective can follow a linking verb: *The sun is warm.*

Interrogative adjectives are used in questions. An interrogative adjective goes before a noun. The interrogative adjectives are *what*, *which*, and *whose*: *What* types of books do you enjoy? *Which* book is your favorite? *Whose* book is this?

Possessive adjectives show possession or ownership. A possessive adjective goes before a noun. The possessive adjectives are *my*, *your* (singular or plural), *his*, *her*, *its*, *our*, and *their*: *his* skateboard, *their* bikes.

Proper adjectives are adjectives that come from proper nouns. A proper adjective begins with a capital letter: *American* history.

Mastery and More

When teachers and students use *Exercises in English,* they receive more than any other language arts workout offers.

Teachers receive MORE with

- easy-to-grade exercises that are always in multiples of five.
- perforated pages for easy grading and portfolio storage.
- embedded answers that make correcting a breeze.

Students receive MORE with

- grammar, mechanics, and usage lessons that support *Voyages in English.*
- cross-curricular content for reinforcement and enrichment in social studies and science.
- character-education lessons with positive role models as examples.
- practice in context for authentic writing opportunities and self-assessment.

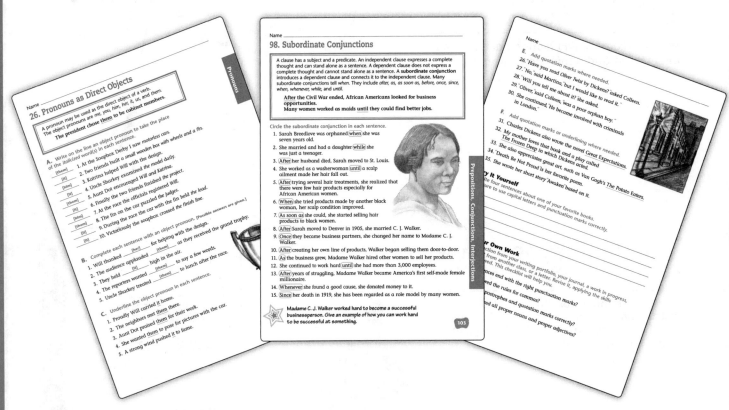

Comprehensive Scope and Sequence

Review the Scope and Sequence on pages T7–T11 to note how skill instruction is scaffolded across levels. Use the level or levels that best meet your students' needs.

Exercises in English—Scope and Sequence

SENTENCES	C	D	E	F	G	H
The Four Kinds of Sentences	✔	✔	✔	✔	✔	✔
Subjects and Predicates	✔	✔	✔	✔	✔	✔
Simple Subjects and Predicates		✔		✔	✔	✔
Compound Subjects and Predicates		✔	✔	✔	✔	✔
Direct Objects		✔	✔	✔	✔	✔
Complete Subjects and Predicates			✔	✔	✔	✔
Natural and Inverted Order in Sentences			✔	✔	✔	✔
Indirect Objects				✔	✔	✔
Compound Sentences				✔	✔	✔
Complex Sentences					✔	✔
Compound Complex Sentences						✔
NOUNS	**C**	**D**	**E**	**F**	**G**	**H**
Proper and Common Nouns	✔	✔	✔	✔	✔	
Singular and Plural Nouns	✔	✔	✔	✔	✔	✔
Possessive Nouns	✔	✔	✔	✔	✔	✔
Nouns Used as Subjects		✔	✔	✔		✔
Nouns Used as Objects		✔	✔	✔	✔	✔
Count and Noncount Nouns		✔	✔	✔		✔
Nouns Used as Subject Complements			✔	✔	✔	✔
Nouns Used in Direct Address			✔	✔		
Nouns Used as Objects of Prepositions			✔	✔	✔	✔
Appositives				✔	✔	✔
Collective Nouns				✔	✔	
Concrete and Abstract Nouns				✔	✔	
Words Used as Nouns and Verbs				✔		
Nouns Used as Object Complements						✔
VERBS	**C**	**D**	**E**	**F**	**G**	**H**
Regular and Irregular Verbs	✔	✔	✔	✔	✔	✔
Present Tense	✔	✔	✔	✔	✔	✔
Progressive Tenses	✔	✔	✔	✔	✔	✔
Past Tense	✔	✔	✔	✔	✔	✔
Future Tenses	✔	✔	✔	✔	✔	✔
Action Verbs	✔	✔	✔			
Verbs of Being	✔	✔	✔			
Helping Verbs	✔	✔				
Forms of *Bring*	✔					

	C	D	E	F	G	H
Forms of *Buy*	✔					
Forms of *Come*	✔					
Forms of *Eat*	✔					
Forms of *Go*	✔		✔			
Forms of *See*	✔		✔			
Forms of *Sit* and *Set*	✔		✔	✔		
Forms of *Take*	✔		✔			
Forms of *Write*	✔					
Forms of *To Be*	✔	✔	✔			
Forms of *Begin*		✔				
Forms of *Break*		✔	✔			
Forms of *Choose*		✔	✔			
Forms of *Do*		✔				
Verb Phrases		✔	✔	✔	✔	
Intransitive Verbs (Linking Verbs)		✔	✔	✔	✔	✔
There Is and *There Are*		✔		✔	✔	
Subject-Verb Agreement			✔	✔	✔	✔
Transitive Verbs			✔	✔	✔	✔
Doesn't and *Don't*			✔	✔	✔	✔
Let and *Leave*			✔	✔		
Teach and *Learn*			✔			
Lie and *Lay*			✔	✔		
Rise and *Raise*				✔		
Perfect Tenses				✔	✔	
Words Used as Nouns and Verbs					✔	
Active and Passive Voice					✔	✔
Modal Auxiliary Verbs					✔	✔
You Are and *You Were*					✔	
Compound Tenses						✔
Emphatic Verb Forms						✔
PRONOUNS	**C**	**D**	**E**	**F**	**G**	**H**
Singular and Plural Pronouns	✔	✔	✔			
Subject Pronouns	✔	✔	✔	✔	✔	✔
Possessive Pronouns	✔	✔	✔	✔	✔	✔
I and *Me*	✔	✔				
Pronouns Used as Subject Complements	✔		✔	✔	✔	✔
Pronouns Used as Direct Objects		✔	✔	✔	✔	✔
The Person of Pronouns		✔	✔	✔		
The Gender of Pronouns			✔			

We and *Us*		✔				
Pronouns Used as Objects of Prepositions			✔	✔		
Pronouns Used in Contractions			✔	✔		
Reflexive Pronouns			✔	✔	✔	
Interrogative Pronouns				✔	✔	✔
Indefinite Pronouns				✔	✔	✔
Double Negatives				✔		
Pronouns Used as Indirect Objects					✔	✔
Who and *Whom*					✔	✔
Pronouns Used After *Than* and *As*					✔	✔
Relative Pronouns					✔	✔
Demonstrative Pronouns					✔	✔
Nothing and *Anything*					✔	
Pronouns Used as Objects of Prepositions						✔
Intensive Pronouns			✔			✔

ADJECTIVES	C	D	E	F	G	H
Descriptive Adjectives	✔			✔	✔	✔
Adjectives That Tell How Many	✔	✔	✔	✔		
Indefinite and Definite Articles	✔	✔	✔	✔	✔	
Demonstrative Adjectives	✔	✔	✔	✔	✔	✔
Comparative Forms of Adjectives	✔	✔	✔	✔	✔	✔
Possessive Adjectives		✔	✔	✔		
Common and Proper Adjectives		✔	✔			✔
Good and *Bad*		✔				
The Position of Adjectives			✔	✔	✔	✔
Superlative Forms of Adjectives			✔	✔	✔	✔
Adjectives Used as Subject Complements				✔		
Words Used as Adjectives or Nouns				✔	✔	✔
Those and *Them*				✔		
Interrogative Adjectives				✔		✔
Few and *Little*					✔	✔

ADVERBS	C	D	E	F	G	H
Adverbs of Time	✔	✔	✔	✔		
Adverbs of Place	✔	✔	✔	✔		
Good and *Well*	✔	✔	✔			
Comparative Adverbs		✔	✔	✔		✔
Adverbs of Manner		✔	✔	✔		
No, Not, and *Never*		✔	✔	✔		
Superlative Adverbs			✔	✔		
Real and *Very*			✔			

	C	D	E	F	G	H
Their and *There*			✔	✔		
To, Too, and *Two*			✔	✔		
Adverbs and Adjectives			✔	✔	✔	
There, Their, and *They're*					✔	
Farther and *Further*					✔	✔
Interrogative Adverbs					✔	✔
Adverbial Nouns					✔	✔
As . . . As, So . . . As, and *Equally*						✔
PUNCTUATION, CAPITALIZATION, ABBREVIATIONS	**C**	**D**	**E**	**F**	**G**	**H**
End Punctuation	✔	✔	✔	✔	✔	✔
Periods After Abbreviations, Titles, and Initials	✔	✔				
Capital Letters	✔	✔	✔	✔	✔	
Titles of Books and Poems	✔		✔	✔	✔	
Commas Used in Direct Address	✔	✔	✔	✔		
Punctuation in Direct Quotations	✔	✔	✔	✔		
Apostrophes		✔	✔			
Commas After *Yes* and *No*		✔	✔	✔		
Commas Separating Words in a Series		✔	✔	✔		
Commas After Parts of a Letter			✔	✔		
Commas in Dates and Addresses			✔	✔		
Commas in Geographical Names			✔			
Commas Used with Appositives				✔		
Commas Used in Compound Sentences				✔		
Semicolons and Colons				✔	✔	✔
Apostrophes, Hyphens, and Dashes				✔	✔	✔
Commas and Semicolons						✔
PREPOSITIONS, CONJUNCTIONS, INTERJECTIONS	**C**	**D**	**E**	**F**	**G**	**. H**
Prepositions and Prepositional Phrases			✔	✔	✔	✔
Interjections			✔	✔	✔	✔
Between and *Among*			✔	✔		
From and *Off*			✔			
Adjectival Phrases			✔			
Adverbial Phrases			✔			
Coordinate Conjunctions			✔			
Words Used as Prepositions and Adverbs				✔	✔	✔
At and *To*				✔		
Beside and *Besides, In* and *Into*				✔		
Coordinate and Correlative Conjunctions					✔	

Conjunctive Adverbs					✔	
Subordinate Conjunctions					✔	✔
Without and *Unless, Like, As,* and *As If*					✔	✔
PHRASES, CLAUSES	C	D	E	F	G	H
Adjectival Phrases				✔	✔	
Adverbial Phrases				✔	✔	
Adjectival Clauses					✔	✔
Adverbial Clauses					✔	✔
Restrictive and Nonrestrictive Clauses					✔	
Noun Clauses						✔
PARTICIPLES, GERUNDS, INFINITIVES	C	D	E	F	G	H
Participles						✔
Dangling Participles						✔
Gerunds						✔
Infinitives						✔
Hidden and Split Infinitives						✔
WORD STUDY SKILLS	C	D	E	F	G	H
Synonyms	✔	✔	✔	✔		
Antonyms	✔	✔				
Homophones	✔	✔	✔			
Contractions	✔	✔				
Compound Words		✔				

Correlation of Grade 5 *Voyages in English, 2006,* and Level E *Exercises in English, 2008*

Exercises in English, 2008

- Grammar is arranged in the same order as in *Voyages,* 2006, allowing students to work through the books simultaneously.

- Each grammar section in *Voyages* is supported by at least one lesson in *Exercises.*

- Some grammar sections in *Voyages* are supported by two or more lessons in *Exercises.* For example, Section 1.6 of *Voyages,* Grade 6, treats nouns used as objects. This section is supported by three lessons in *Exercises* that treat separately nouns used as direct objects, nouns used as indirect objects, and nouns used as objects of prepositions. This gives students extra practice in discrete grammar points.

- The grammar explanations in *Exercises* were rewritten to match those in *Voyages,* making it easy to move back and forth between books.

- An entire chapter of diagramming was added to *Exercises* to match that in *Voyages.* (This replaces the old Research Skills section. Research skills are taught in *Voyages* as part of the writing process, not as part of the grammar.)

- The Handbook of Terms for each level was rewritten to match that of *Voyages.*

- The TE front matter now contains a correlation of *Exercises* with the appropriate grade level of *Voyages.* (This replaces the old Sentence Analysis section.)

Features that were retained from the old *Exercises* include:

- Each exercise is based on grade-level science, social studies, or language arts content.

- The items in each exercise are divisible by 5 for easy grading.

- Character education lessons appear throughout each book.

- Section reviews provide regular assessment.

- Writing in context and self-assessment allow students to practice what they learn and to evaluate their own work.

- The TE contains overprinted answers.

- The TE front matter contains a scope and sequence chart of the entire program.

Grammar Workbook

EXERCISES
in ENGLISH

LEVEL E

LOYOLAPRESS.

CHICAGO

Consultants

Therese Elizabeth Bauer
Martina Anne Erdlen
Anita Patrick Gallagher
Patricia Healey
Irene Kervick
Susan Platt

Linguistics Advisor

Timothy G. Collins
National-Louis University

Series Design: Loyola Press
Interior Art:
Jim Mitchell: 18, 24, 43, 68, 80, 86, 97, 103, 109, 120.
Greg Phillips: 16, 49, 51, 64, 112, 118, 123.
All interior illustrations not listed above are by Stacy Previn/munrocampagna.com.

ISBN-10: 0-8294-2343-5; ISBN-13: 978-0-8294-2343-3

ISBN-10: 0-8294-2337-0; ISBN-13: 978-0-8294-2337-2

Exercises in English® is a registered trademark of Loyola Press.

Manufactured in the United States of America.

06 07 08 09 10 11 12 VonH 10 9 8 7 6 5 4 3 2 1

06 07 08 09 10 11 12 VonH 10 9 8 7 6 5 4 3 2 1

Contents

1. Nouns

> A **noun** is a name word. A noun names a person, a place, or a thing.
>
> **hiker   campground   tent**

A. The following words are nouns. Write each in the proper column.

	PERSON	PLACE	THING
1. uncles	[uncles]		
2. Los Angeles		[Los Angeles]	
3. keys			[keys]
4. dashboard			[dashboard]
5. children	[children]		
6. Walbridge Park		[Walbridge Park]	
7. William	[William]		
8. streetlight			[streetlight]
9. Cleveland		[Cleveland]	
10. automobile			[automobile]

B. Underline the nouns in each sentence. The number of nouns in each sentence is in parentheses.

1. <u>Mildred Taylor</u> wrote a <u>book</u> called *The Gold Cadillac.* (3)
2. The <u>father</u> in the <u>story</u> bought an expensive <u>car</u>. (3)
3. His <u>wife</u> had wanted to save <u>money</u> for a <u>house</u>. (3)
4. The <u>father</u> and the <u>children</u> drove to <u>Detroit</u> to visit <u>relatives</u>. (4)
5. The <u>mother</u> refused to go and decided to stay at <u>home</u>. (2)

C. Complete each sentence with nouns. [Answers will vary.]

1. The next trip was to _____ and _____.
2. They stopped at a _____ and a _____.
3. The family spoke to a _____ and a _____.
4. They stayed at a _____ and a _____.
5. The children brought home a _____ and a _____.

2. Common Nouns and Proper Nouns

Nouns

> There are two main kinds of nouns: common nouns and proper nouns.
>
> A **common noun** names any one member of a group of persons, places, or things.
>
>   queen   city   church
>
> A **proper noun** names a particular person, place, or thing.
>
>   **Queen Elizabeth**   **London**   **Westminster Abbey**

A. Circle each common noun. Underline each proper noun.

1. Japan gave the United States some trees.

2. These trees were planted around the Tidal Basin in Washington, D.C.

3. Beautiful flowers bloom on these trees in April.

4. The blossoms are pink and white.

5. The flowers last for only 10 to 12 days.

6. Photographers from many countries take pictures of the blossoms.

7. The Jefferson Memorial is also decorated by these beautiful flowers.

8. In Japan the people have a festival when the first buds appear.

9. Washington, D.C., holds an annual Cherry Blossom Festival.

10. The United States received a beautiful gift from the people of Japan.

B. Complete each sentence with a proper noun to match the common noun in parentheses.

1. My Uncle Mike bought a new _____[Answers will vary.]_____. (car)

2. Jessica shopped at _____ for the gift. (store)

3. We went to _____ for our vacation. (place)

4. After the game _____ treated us to a hamburger. (person)

5. Carlos read _____ for one hour. (book)

3. More Common Nouns and Proper Nouns

A. Write a common noun for each proper noun. **[Answers will vary. Samples are given.]**

	COMMON NOUN		COMMON NOUN
1. Canada	[country]	11. Boston	[city]
2. Brian	[boy]	12. Earth	[planet]
3. Florida	[state]	13. Sunday	[day]
4. March	[month]	14. Alps	[mountains]
5. Donald Duck	[cartoon character]	15. Pacific Ocean	[ocean]
6. North America	[continent]	16. Abraham Lincoln	[president]
7. Thanksgiving	[holiday]	17. Memorial Day	[holiday]
8. Beverly Cleary	[author]	18. Thomas Edison	[inventor]
9. Brown University	[school]	19. Buick	[car]
10. Joe's Diner	[restaurant]	20. Mississippi River	[river]

B. Write a proper noun suggested by each common noun. **[Answers will vary.]**

	PROPER NOUN		PROPER NOUN
1. man	_____	11. mountains	_____
2. country	_____	12. ocean	_____
3. singer	_____	13. statue	_____
4. president	_____	14. general	_____
5. astronaut	_____	15. car	_____
6. holiday	_____	16. inventor	_____
7. comic strip	_____	17. street	_____
8. lake	_____	18. store	_____
9. detective	_____	19. movie star	_____
10. game	_____	20. restaurant	_____

C. Complete the sentences with proper nouns. **[Answers will vary.]**

In _____ my family visited _____ during the _____
      1. month   2. place   3. holiday

weekend. My friend _____ came with us. I saw _____ for the
               4. person   5. thing

first time.

Name _____

4. Singular Nouns and Plural Nouns

A **singular noun** tells about one person, place, or thing. A **plural noun** tells about more than one. The plural of most nouns is made by adding -*s* or -*es* to the singular form. For nouns ending in *y* after a consonant, change the *y* to *i* and add -*es*. For some nouns ending in *f* or *fe,* change the *f* or *fe* to *v* and add -*es*.

SINGULAR	PLURAL	SINGULAR	PLURAL	SINGULAR	PLURAL
nut	nuts	day	days	roof	roofs
bench	benches	berry	berries	wolf	wolves

Complete the letter by writing the correct plural forms of the nouns in parentheses.

Dear Mom and Dad,

I love visiting Uncle Ted and Aunt Maki

on their farm. One day we picked ____[peaches]____
1. peach

and ____[cherries]____. The fruit was so ripe that
2. cherry

we just shook the ____[branches]____, and the fruit
3. branch

and ____[leaves]____ fell off the ____[trees]____. We had ____[bushels]____! The
4. leaf   5. tree   6. bushel

fruit was then packed in ____[boxes]____ and shipped to ____[factories]____ where it
7. box   8. factory

will be made into jam. Soon the ____[jars]____ will appear on our supermarket
9. jar

____[shelves]____!
10. shelf

Later in the week, Ted and I paddled ____[kayaks]____ down the stream.
11. kayak

We saw two mother ____[foxes]____ with their ____[babies]____. I was really
12. fox   13. baby

surprised. I never expected to see wild ____[animals]____ so close to the farm.
14. animal

I've been helping Aunt Maki a lot too. I get ____[vegetables]____ for dinner right
15. vegetable

out of the garden. We have fresh ____[carrots]____, ____[radishes]____, and
16. carrot   17. radish

____[cucumbers]____ every night. After dinner I help her do the ____[dishes]____.
18. cucumber   19. dish

This trip has been my favorite of all my ____[vacations]____!
20. vacation

Love,

Joey

4

5. More Singular Nouns and Plural Nouns

> For nouns ending in *o* after a vowel, form the plural by adding *-s* to the singular form. For some nouns ending in *o* after a consonant, add *-es* to the singular. Some singular nouns use a different word to show the plural. Some nouns use the same word for the singular and the plural.
>
> | SINGULAR | PLURAL | SINGULAR | PLURAL | SINGULAR | PLURAL |
> |----------|--------|----------|--------|----------|--------|
> | radio | radios | goose | geese | deer | deer |
> | tomato | tomatoes | man | men | salmon | salmon |
> | trio | trios | tooth | teeth | series | series |

A. Write the correct plural form for each noun.

1. child   [children]
2. bison   [bison]
3. piano   [pianos]
4. potato   [potatoes]
5. mouse   [mice]
6. ox   [oxen]
7. hero   [heroes]
8. trout   [trout]
9. species   [species]
10. moose   [moose]

B. Complete each sentence with the plural form of the noun. Use a capital letter when necessary.

1. ranch   Cowhands work on ___[ranches]___ in the American West.
2. burro   They ride horses and use mules and ___[burros]___ as pack animals.
3. lasso   Cowhands use their ___[lassos]___ to catch stray cattle.
4. wolf   They protect cattle from predators such as pumas and ___[wolves]___.
5. calf   They brand ___[calves]___ with the ranch's brand.
6. sombrero   Early cowhands wore ___[sombreros]___.
7. sheep   Some ranchers raise ___[sheep]___ instead of cattle.
8. rodeo   Many cowhands compete in ___[rodeos]___.
9. bronco   Men ride bulls and bucking ___[broncos]___.
10. woman   ___[Women]___ compete in events such as barrel racing.

6. Possessive Nouns

The **possessive form** of a noun expresses possession or ownership. The apostrophe (') is the sign of a possessive noun. To form the possessive of a singular noun, add -'s to the singular form.

> architect   architect's

To form the possessive of a plural noun that ends in -s, add an apostrophe (') to the plural form.

> farmers   farmers'

To form the possessive of a plural noun that does not end in -s, add -'s to the plural form.

> children   children's

A. Rewrite the following, using singular possessive nouns.

1. the whistle of the referee   [the referee's whistle]

2. the voice of the coach   [the coach's voice]

3. the horse of Paul Revere   [Paul Revere's horse]

4. the badge of the officer   [the officer's badge]

5. the spurs of the cowboy   [the cowboy's spurs]

B. Rewrite the following, using plural possessive nouns.

1. the cries of the babies   [the babies' cries]

2. the suggestions of both men   [both men's suggestions]

3. the wishbones of the turkeys   [the turkeys' wishbones]

4. the carts of the golfers   [the golfers' carts]

5. the tractors of the farmers   [the farmers' tractors]

C. Underline the correct possessive form of the noun in each sentence.

1. The circus (<u>ringmaster's</u> ringmasters') voice announced the next act.

2. A (<u>lion's</u> lions') roar caused excitement.

3. All of the (elephant's <u>elephants'</u>) tails had pink bows on them.

4. All of the (child's <u>children's</u>) eyes followed the tightrope walker.

5. One (<u>acrobat's</u> acrobats') trick amazed everyone.

7. More Possessive Nouns

> A noun has both a singular and a plural possessive form.

A. Write the singular possessive and the plural possessive of each noun.

	SINGULAR POSSESSIVE	PLURAL POSSESSIVE
1. doctor	[doctor's]	[doctors']
2. baby	[baby's]	[babies']
3. wolf	[wolf's]	[wolves']
4. child	[child's]	[children's]
5. fox	[fox's]	[foxes']

B. Complete each sentence with the possessive form of the noun. Use a capital letter when necessary.

national parks   1. Grizzly bears are one of the [national parks'] protected species.

Alaska   2. One of [Alaska's] claims to fame is the grizzly, a type of brown bear.

grizzlies   3. [Grizzlies'] bodies are massive, sometimes measuring eight feet long and weighing as much as 900 pounds.

cubs   4. A grizzly's den may contain cubs and the [cubs'] food.

bear   5. This [bear's] claws are straight and not good for climbing.

camper   6. Every [camper's] fear is to encounter a grizzly.

food   7. [Food's] presence at a campsite can attract a bear.

human   8. A [human's] response to seeing a grizzly can range from excitement to terror.

nature   9. Another of [nature's] wild creatures is the puma.

puma   10. The [puma's] many other names include catamount, panther, and mountain lion.

jungle   11. The puma is among the [jungle's] inhabitants, but it is also found in mountains and deserts.

kittens   12. Its [kittens'] behavior is very playful.

cat   13. A domestic [cat's] instincts are similar to a puma's.

deer   14. Many [deer's] lives have been cut short by hungry pumas.

hunters   15. [Hunters'] means of catching pumas are traps and open pits.

8. Collective Nouns, Count and Noncount Nouns

> A **collective noun** names a group of persons, places, or things that are considered as a unit.
> **The cast and the orchestra bowed to the audience.**
>
> **Count nouns** name items that can be counted separately. Count nouns have singular and plural forms.
> **The students and the teachers worked on the projects.**
>
> **Noncount nouns** name items that cannot be counted separately. They usually do not have plural forms, and they generally take singular verbs.
> **Lemonade is made from sugar, water, and juice.**

A. Write a collective noun for each word. **[Answers may vary.]**

1. cows _____[herd]_____
2. geese _____[flock]_____
3. members _____[club]_____
4. actors _____[cast]_____
5. musicians _____[band]_____
6. bees _____[swarm]_____
7. scouts _____[troop]_____
8. singers _____[chorus]_____
9. bananas _____[bunch]_____
10. wolves _____[pack]_____

B. Circle each count noun. Underline each noncount noun.

1. It's easy to turn raw (vegetables) into delicious soup.
2. Heat two (tablespoons) of oil in a large (pot).
3. Chop one large (onion) and three (stalks) of celery and cook them in the hot oil.
4. Stir in one (cup) of sliced (carrots) and one large, chopped (potato).
5. Add one small, sliced (zucchini) and one medium-sized (can) of diced (tomatoes).
6. Slowly pour in six (cups) of stock or water.
7. Reduce the heat and cook for 15 to 20 (minutes).
8. When the (potatoes) and (carrots) are tender, add one-half (cup) of pasta.
9. Stir in one (box) of frozen (peas) and one (bunch) of chopped parsley.
10. Taste the soup and add salt and pepper as needed.
11. Serve salad and some crusty bread for a perfect (meal).
12. Shred one large (head) of lettuce and put it into a (bowl).
13. Drain one (can) of (artichokes) and add them to the lettuce.
14. Sprinkle on some cheese.
15. Serve with oil and vinegar.

Name _____

9. Nouns as Subjects

> A sentence has a subject and a predicate. The **simple subject** is usually the noun that names the person, place, or thing the sentence is about.
>
> **The brave <u>firefighters</u> rushed into the burning building.**

A. Underline the simple subject in each sentence.

1. Many <u>tribes</u> lived along the Atlantic coastline.

2. These <u>Native Americans</u> had lived there long before the arrival of Europeans.

3. <u>Villages</u> were located near lakes and rivers.

4. Six large <u>tribes</u> lived in the area from Canada to Florida.

5. Each <u>tribe</u> was an independent nation.

6. Some <u>tribes</u> had leaders called sachems.

7. A tribe's <u>sachem</u> could be a man or a woman.

8. A <u>council</u> of village leaders served with the chief.

9. The first <u>colonists</u> were helped by these Native Americans.

10. <u>Chief Massasoit</u> aided the Pilgrims.

B. Complete each sentence with a subject noun. Use each noun only once.

queen	island	Arthur	knights	sword
legend	king	wife	stone	court

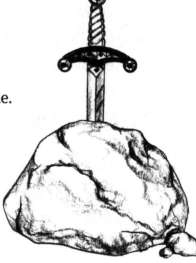

1. King Arthur's __[sword]__ was named Excalibur.

2. A large __[stone]__ had the sword stuck into it.

3. __[Arthur]__ alone was able to pull the sword out of the stone.

4. The __[court]__ of King Arthur was at Camelot.

5. Brave __[knights]__ such as Sir Lancelot attended the court.

6. The __[wife]__ of King Arthur was named Guinevere.

7. The __[queen]__ fell in love with Sir Lancelot.

8. One __[legend]__ tells about Arthur's sister, Morgan le Fay.

9. The __[island]__ of Avalon was ruled by Morgan le Fay.

10. The __[king]__ went to his sister's island to be healed of his wounds.

10. Nouns as Subject Complements

Nouns

> A **subject complement** is often a noun. It renames the subject and completes the meaning of a linking verb in a sentence.
>
> SUBJECT   SUBJECT COMPLEMENT
> **Debbie is a fitness instructor.**

A. Circle the simple subject in each sentence. Underline the subject complement.

1. (Snoopy) is a black-and-white beagle.
2. (Charlie Brown) is the owner of Snoopy.
3. (Woodstock) is a small yellow bird.
4. (Woodstock) is Snoopy's friend.
5. In the winter (Woodstock) is a hockey player on his frozen birdbath.
6. In the summer the (birdbath) is Woodstock's swimming pool.
7. (Snoopy) is a baseball player too.
8. (Charlie Brown) is the manager of the baseball team.
9. The other (players) are friends of Charlie Brown.
10. (Charles Schulz) was the creator of all these characters.

B. Complete each sentence with a noun used as a subject complement.

1. A famous school is _____ [Answers will vary.] _____ .
2. In school my favorite subject is _____ .
3. My teacher is _____ .
4. The student across from me is _____ .
5. In our school the principal is _____ .

C. Complete each sentence with the correct subject complement.

capital   name   Dairy State   bird   range

1. Wisconsin is the ____[Dairy State]____ .
2. Denver is the ____[capital]____ of Colorado.
3. The Sierra Nevada is a mountain ____[range]____ .
4. Missouri is the ____[name]____ of both a state and a river.
5. The cardinal is the state ____[bird]____ of seven states.

11. Nouns as Direct Objects

> The **direct object** answers the question *whom* or *what* after an action verb in a sentence.
>
> **After waiting in line for hours, we managed to purchase two tickets for the show.**
> (*Tickets* answers the question *what—What* did we manage to purchase?)
>
> **The show stars my favorite singer.**
> (*Singer* answers the question *whom—Whom* does the show star?)

A. Circle the direct object in each sentence. Write on the line whether it answers the question *whom* or *what*.

[whom] 1. Connecticut claims two famous (men) from the American Revolution.

[whom] 2. The state honors (Nathan Hale) as a hero.

[what] 3. At first Nathan Hale taught (school.)

[what] 4. Hale joined the (army) of George Washington.

[what] 5. Washington needed (information) about the British troops.

[what] 6. In his schoolmaster's clothes Hale crossed the British (lines.)

[what] 7. On the British side Hale drew (maps) of the British locations.

[what] 8. He hid the (maps) and (information) in his shoes.

[whom] 9. Unfortunately, a British soldier recognized (Hale.)

[whom] 10. The British hanged (Nathan Hale) for spying.

B. Complete each sentence with a direct object. Use each noun once.

battles	information	forts	town	marks
traitor	soldier	sides	hero	Benedict Arnold

1. Connecticut also produced a _____[traitor]_____.

2. Americans remember ___[Benedict Arnold]___ as a spy.

3. General Arnold first won _____[battles]_____ for the Americans.

4. Benedict Arnold changed _____[sides]_____ during the war, however.

5. This traitor leaked _____[information]_____ to the British.

6. For the British, General Arnold captured two American _____[forts]_____.

7. During battle Arnold's troops killed every _____[soldier]_____ in one fort.

8. His troops also burned the _____[town]_____ of Griswald.

9. After the war Britain accepted its _____[hero]_____ as a citizen.

10. Nathan Hale and Benedict Arnold left their _____[marks]_____ on history.

Nouns

Name _____

12. Direct Objects and Subject Complements

Read each sentence. Write DO on the line if the *italicized* word is a direct object. Write SC if it is a subject complement.

[SC] 1. Tropical rain forests are the earth's oldest living *ecosystems*.

[DO] 2. Rain forests cover only a small *part* of the earth's surface.

[SC] 3. They are *home* to half the plant and animal species on the earth.

[DO] 4. Torrential rains have washed most *nutrients* from the soil.

[DO] 5. Rain forests have no dry or cold *seasons*.

[DO] 6. A tropical rain forest has four *layers*.

[SC] 7. The emergent layer is the tallest *layer* in a rain forest.

[DO] 8. The canopy contains the most *food* for rain forest animals.

[DO] 9. The emergent layer and the canopy receive the most *sunshine*.

[SC] 10. Most rain forest animals are *inhabitants* of the top layers.

[SC] 11. The fourth layer of a rain forest is the *understory*.

[DO] 12. Tree roots, soil, and decaying material constitute the forest *floor*.

[DO] 13. The understory and the forest floor receive very little *light*.

[SC] 14. Large animals are *residents* of the forest floor.

[SC] 15. Foods such as bananas, chocolate, and pepper are *products* of rain forests.

[SC] 16. These foods are maintainable *resources*.

[DO] 17. The Amazon rain forest covers an *area* about two thirds the size of the continental United States.

[SC] 18. It is the world's largest *rain forest*.

[DO] 19. Rain forests help control the world's *climate*.

[DO] 20. Rain forests affect all *human beings* on earth.

12

13. Objects of Prepositions

> **Prepositions** can show place, time, direction, and relationship. Some common prepositions are *in, into, on, to, by, for, from, at, of, with,* and *without.*
> A **prepositional phrase** consists of a preposition and its object, a noun or a pronoun. The noun or the pronoun that follows the preposition is called the **object of the preposition.**
>
> **The group of fans cheered at the appearance of the singer.**

A. Underline the prepositions in the sentences. Circle the object of each preposition. Some sentences have more than one prepositional phrase.

1. The bat hangs upside-down in its (cave.)
2. The sharp claws on its (toes) cling to the (ceiling.)
3. Bats sleep in this (position.)
4. At (night) the bat awakes.
5. Its lips push into the (shape) of a (horn.)
6. Squeaking sounds come from its (throat.)
7. The noise vibrates the air in the (cave.)
8. The bat listens for (echoes) from its (squeaks.)
9. From the (echoes,) the bat can "see" anything in the (dark.)
10. Bats are not blind in the (daylight.)

B. Complete the paragraph by adding objects of the prepositions. Add words if necessary. [Answers will vary.]

My friends dared me, so I walked into (1.) _____. The insides were

covered with (2.)_____, but I kept walking. Soon I heard sounds

from (3.) _____. I felt a chill run down (4.) _____. I had

a lump in (5.) _____. My feet were stuck to (6.) _____.

Suddenly I felt a cold hand on (7.) _____. A cry finally came from

(8.) _____. Turning around, I saw a man with (9.) _____

in (10.) _____.

C. Write one or two sentences to finish the paragraph.

_____

_____

_____

14. Nouns as Indirect Objects

> The **indirect object** in a sentence tells *to whom, to what, for whom,* or *for what* the action was done. The indirect object comes between the verb and the direct object.
>
> | VERB | INDIRECT OBJECT | DIRECT OBJECT |
> |------|-----------------|---------------|
> | Sylvia <u>brought</u> | **Karen** | <u>souvenirs</u> from her trip to Egypt. |

A. Circle the indirect object in each sentence. The direct object is *italicized*.

1. The Amendments to the Constitution give (Americans) certain *rights*.

2. The First Amendment guarantees (people) *freedom* of speech and religion.

3. The Fourth Amendment assures (residents) *security* against illegal searches.

4. The Sixth Amendment promises an accused (person) a speedy *trial*.

5. The Eighth Amendment gives (citizens) *protection* against cruel and unusual punishment.

6. The Thirteenth Amendment offered (slaves) their *freedom*.

7. The Fifteenth Amendment promised African American (males) the *vote*.

8. The Nineteenth Amendment gave (women) the *right* to vote.

9. The Twenty-second Amendment denies a (leader) a third *term* as president.

10. The Twenty-sixth Amendment assures (18-year-olds) the *vote*.

B. Underline the direct object in each sentence. Circle the indirect object.

1. Mr. Rosenbaum assigned the (class) a <u>project</u> on the Constitution.

2. He offered the (students) any <u>help</u> they needed.

3. Maya read a small (group) the <u>Bill of Rights</u>.

4. Michael showed his (partner) a <u>Web site</u> about the Constitutional Convention.

5. Carl and Anna sent their (senator) a <u>request</u> for an interview.

6. Mr. Rosenbaum lent (Laura) a <u>biography</u> of Thomas Jefferson.

7. Tricia handed (Mr. Rosenbaum) her <u>paper</u> about John Adams.

8. Oscar told his (classmates) a <u>story</u> about Benjamin Franklin.

9. The principal promised the fifth (grade) a <u>trip</u> to Philadelphia.

10. The children sold their (neighbors) <u>candy</u> to pay for the trip.

15. Nouns in Direct Address

> A noun is used in direct address when it names the person spoken to.
> **Doctor, do you think I have pneumonia?**

A. Underline the noun(s) in direct address in each sentence.

1. <u>Folks</u>, step right up and get your tickets.
2. Be careful, <u>boys</u>, going down the steps.
3. These are box seats, <u>Dad</u>!
4. <u>Mr. Martinez</u>, do you think we will be able to get autographs?
5. Maybe, <u>Jim</u>, we might get a few.
6. <u>Fans</u>, please stand for the national anthem.
7. Step up to the plate, <u>batter</u>.
8. I don't think that was a strike, <u>Dad</u>!
9. <u>Jim</u> and <u>Todd</u>, do you want hot dogs?
10. Do you want mustard, <u>boys</u>, on the hot dogs?

B. Complete each sentence with a noun in direct address.

Mrs. Velez   Nurse Higgens   Coach   Rosa   Doctor

1. Where does your arm hurt, ____[Rosa]____?
2. Bring me Rosa's chart, ____[Nurse Higgens]____.
3. ____[Doctor]____, is my arm broken?
4. ____[Mrs. Velez]____, your daughter will need a cast for six weeks.
5. I won't be able to play in the game on Saturday, ____[Coach]____.

C. Write sentences, using each word as a noun in direct address.
Vary the position of the noun. **[Sentences will vary.]**

José   1. _____

Laura   2. _____

class   3. _____

Coach   4. _____

swimmers   5. _____

Nouns

16. Words Used as Nouns or as Verbs

A noun is a naming word. A verb expresses action or being.
Many words can be used either as nouns or as verbs.

VERB   NOUN

Be careful when you <u>step</u> on that crooked <u>step</u>.

A. Write **N** if the *italicized* word is a noun. Write **V** if it is a verb.

_[V]_ 1. We often *visit* Philadelphia.

_[V]_ 2. You should *plan* to go there.

_[N]_ 3. A *visit* to Independence Hall is interesting.

_[N]_ 4. Alexander Hamilton oversaw the *plan* for the Hall.

_[V]_ 5. The delegates *debated* about the wording of the U.S. Constitution.

_[N]_ 6. George Washington presided over the *debate*.

_[N]_ 7. From Independence Hall it's just a short *walk* to the Liberty Bell.

_[V]_ 8. Did the bell *crack* the first time it was rung?

_[N]_ 9. The *crack* is about two feet long.

_[V]_ 10. Next *walk* down the street to Betsy Ross's house.

B. Write sentences, using each word first as a noun and then as a verb.

1. design   **[Answers will vary.]** _____

_____

2. rule   _____

_____

3. surprise _____

_____

4. judge   _____

_____

5. ring   _____

_____

Name _____

17. Words Used as Nouns or as Adjectives

A noun is a naming word. An adjective describes a noun. Many words can be used either as nouns or as adjectives.

ADJECTIVE   NOUN
The <u>football</u> coach tossed Jason the <u>football</u>.

Nouns

A. Write N if the *italicized* word is a noun. Write A if it is an adjective.

__[N]__ 1. George Washington Carver was born a *slave* in 1864.

__[A]__ 2. When he was a boy, *slave* traders kidnapped him and his mother.

__[N]__ 3. He worked on a *farm* while he went to high school.

__[N]__ 4. When he was 30, he went to *college* in Iowa.

__[A]__ 5. Then he became a *college* professor.

__[A]__ 6. He started studying the diseases of *farm* crops.

__[A]__ 7. *Peanut* plants enrich the soil in which they are grown.

__[N]__ 8. Carver is famous for inventing many uses for the *peanut*.

__[A]__ 9. *Cotton* plantations were turned into peanut farms.

__[N]__ 10. *Cotton* was no longer the main crop raised in the South.

B. Write sentences, using each term first as a noun and then as an adjective.

1. bicycle   [Answers will vary.] _____

_____

2. cell phone _____

_____

3. soccer _____

_____

4. truck _____

_____

5. pencil _____

_____

17

Name _____

18. Uses of Nouns

Nouns can be used in different ways.

S	subject	The doctor wrote the prescription.
SC	subject complement	She is a surgeon.
DO	direct object	She has a degree from Harvard University.
IO	indirect object	She gives her patients a lot of attention.
OP	object of a preposition	She practices with several doctors.
DA	direct address	Doctor, do I have a fever?

Underline each noun. Above each noun write its use. Use the letters given in the box above.

      [DA]   **[OP]**
1. Shelly, did you vote in the election?

        [DA]   **[DO]**
2. Yes, Erica, I cast my ballot.

    [S]   **[DO]**   **[OP]**
3. Women didn't always have the right to vote in the United States.

            [DO]   **[OP]**   **[OP]**
4. They gained this right in 1920 through the Nineteenth Amendment.

       [S]   **[OP]**
5. Susan B. Anthony fought for this right.

        [IO]   **[DO]**
6. She gave Congress her opinions.

        [S]   **[DO]**
7. She and a friend published a newspaper.

     [S]   **[OP]**   **[SC]**
8. The name of their paper was *The Revolution.*

     [S]   **[IO]**   **[DO]**   **[OP]**   **[OP]**
9. The paper gave readers a different view on issues of the day.

      [S]   **[OP]**   **[OP]**
10. Susan B. Anthony also worked for a change in women's fashion.

        [DO]
11. She cut her hair short.

        [DO]   **[OP]**
12. She even wore a type of pants.

     [S]   **[OP]**
13. Many people did not approve of this attire.

     [S]   **[DO]**
14. Women should thank Susan B. Anthony.

        [SC]   **[OP]**
15. She was a tireless worker for the rights of all.

 Susan B. Anthony fought for women's causes. Give an example of how you can help a cause that you believe in.

18

19. Reviewing Nouns

A. Write on the line whether the *italicized* noun is a count noun or a noncount noun.

___[count]___ 1. French *citizens* gave the United States a gift in 1884.

___[count]___ 2. This *gift* was the Statue of Liberty.

___[noncount]___ 3. This monument was a sign of friendship and *liberty*.

___[count]___ 4. Édouard de Laboulaye, a *historian*, suggested the idea.

___[noncount]___ 5. The people of France donated *money* for the statue.

B. Write on the line whether the *italicized* noun is common or proper.

___[proper]___ 6. *Frédéric Auguste Bartholdi* designed the statue.

___[common]___ 7. The statue was to be built as a proud *woman*.

___[common]___ 8. Her *crown* was made with seven spikes.

___[common]___ 9. The spikes represented the world's seven seas and *continents*.

___[proper]___ 10. She holds a book with the date of the *Declaration of Independence* on it.

C. Write on the line whether the *italicized* noun is the subject, the direct object, or the object of a preposition.

___[subject]___ 11. The *engineer* of the statue was Alexandre Gustave Eiffel.

___[direct object]___ 12. Eiffel built the *skeleton* for the copper body.

___[object of a preposition]___ 13. Sheets of copper were hammered onto the *frame*.

___[subject]___ 14. Bartholdi's *mother* was the model for the face.

___[direct object]___ 15. The two men shared their *talents* with the United States.

D. Circle the subject in each sentence. Draw a line under the subject complement.

16. The (statue) is a female figure 151 feet tall.

17. The (base) of the statue is a pedestal 154 feet high.

18. The (crown) of the statue was once an observation deck.

19. The (lights) in the torch are powerful electric lamps.

20. The (home) for this great lady is New York Harbor.

CONTINUED

Name _____

E. Circle the noun in direct address in each sentence.

21. (Dad,) do we really own that red convertible?

22. Yes, we sure do, (Danielle.)

23. Would you like to go for a ride, (girls)?

24. Do you want to come along, (Grandma)?

25. Sure. (Molly,) would you get my purse?

F. Write on the line whether the *italicized* noun is a direct object, an indirect object, or a subject complement.

_____[subject complement]_____ 26. Our last car was a *sedan*.

_____[direct object]_____ 27. Dad bought the *convertible* from a nearby dealer.

_____[direct object]_____ 28. It has leather *seats*.

_____[subject complement]_____ 29. The car is a beautiful *machine*.

_____[indirect object]_____ 30. Dad gave *Mom* a wonderful surprise.

Try It Yourself
Write four sentences about a place you know. Think about your use of nouns.
Check your spelling of proper, plural, and possessive nouns.

_____

_____

_____

_____

Check Your Own Work
Choose a selection from your writing portfolio, your journal,
a work in progress, an assignment from another class, or a letter.
Revise it, applying the skills you have reviewed. This checklist will help you.

✔ Have you capitalized all proper nouns?

✔ Have you used the correct plural forms?

✔ Have you used the apostrophe correctly?

✔ Have you chosen nouns that create a word picture?

Name _____

20. Singular Pronouns and Plural Pronouns

> A **pronoun** takes the place of a noun. A **personal pronoun** changes form depending on to whom or what it refers and to the role it plays in a sentence.
>
> **The fishermen hauled in the net.**   **Mrs. Murphy teaches school.**
> **They hauled in the net.**   **She teaches school.**
>
> A personal pronoun is singular when it refers to one person, place, or thing.
>
> **He is a computer whiz.**
>
> A personal pronoun is plural when it refers to more than one person, place, or thing.
>
> **We were caught in a torrential downpour.**

A. Write **S** on the line if the *italicized* pronoun in each sentence is singular or **P** if it is plural.

__[P]__ 1. Our teacher read *us* a story about Harry S Truman.

__[S]__ 2. *It* was from a biography by David R. Collins.

__[S]__ 3. *I* saw the book in the library once.

__[S]__ 4. Mrs. Raul read *it* to us a chapter at a time.

__[S]__ 5. *She* always waited until after recess.

__[P]__ 6. *We* could hardly wait to hear about Harry.

__[S]__ 7. The Bowman twins like the part about *him* on the farm.

__[P]__ 8. *They* lived on a farm too.

__[P]__ 9. The Truman family owned cows; Harry milked *them*.

__[S]__ 10. *He* had other chores to do also.

B. Write a pronoun to take the place of the *italicized* words.

1. *The Truman children* worked hard on the farm.

   ___[They]___ worked hard on the farm.

2. Early each morning *Harry* went to the barn.

   Early each morning ___[he]___ went to the barn.

3. He walked *the goats* to the public spring.

   He walked ___[them]___ to the public spring.

4. Mrs. Truman raised chickens in *a large hen house*.

   Mrs. Truman raised chickens in ___[it]___ .

5. Every day *Vivian* gathered eggs from the hens.

   Every day ___[she]___ gathered eggs from the hens.

21. Personal Pronouns

A personal pronoun names the speaker; the person spoken to; or the person, place, or thing spoken about.

The personal pronouns that name the speaker are *I, me, mine, we, us,* and *ours.* (first person)

> **I wish the weather would change.**   **The book was a gift to <u>me</u>.**
> **<u>We</u> wish Ming would stop by.**   **Sue and Harry waited for <u>us</u>.**

The personal pronouns that name the person spoken to are *you* and *yours.* (second person)

> **Why don't <u>you</u> borrow my umbrella?**

The personal pronouns that name the person, place, or thing spoken about are *he, she, it, him, her, his, hers, its, they, them,* and *theirs.* (third person)

> **<u>He</u> spent all the money.**   **Give the present to <u>him</u>.**
> **<u>She</u> brought the fish to school.**   **Sarah would like to see <u>hers</u>.**
> **<u>They</u> always make a lot of noise.**   **Does the officer believe <u>them</u>?**

A. Underline the personal pronoun(s) that names the speaker.

1. Thoughtfully <u>I</u> waited on the stage for the spelling bee to begin.

2. <u>We</u> were all a bit nervous.

3. My teacher smiled encouragingly at <u>me</u>.

4. The judges gave <u>us</u> time to think.

5. As the words were given, <u>I</u> waited for <u>mine</u>.

B. Underline the personal pronoun(s) that names the person spoken to.

1. Have <u>you</u> ever been in that position?

2. <u>You</u> should try facing an audience!

3. Looking at them, <u>you</u> can feel everyone is pulling for <u>you</u>.

4. It is scary when <u>yours</u> is the first word announced.

5. Could <u>you</u> spell that word?

C. Underline the personal pronoun(s) that names the person or thing spoken about.

1. Joe was very nervous; <u>he</u> knew <u>his</u> would be the first word.

2. The crowd waited with <u>him</u>.

3. <u>They</u> all missed the same word that Joe missed.

4. Not one of <u>them</u> could spell the word.

5. Joe knew how to spell the next word, and <u>he</u> won the contest.

Name _____

22. More Personal Pronouns

> A pronoun can be in the first, second, or third person.
> The third person singular pronoun can refer to a male, a female, or a thing.
>
> **He** made lunch today. (third person, male)
> **She** set the table. (third person, female)
> **It** was beautiful. (third person, thing)

A. Write **1** above the personal pronouns that are in the first person. Write **2** above the pronouns in the second person. Write **3** above the pronouns in the third person.

1. [1] We want to give [3] her a present.
2. [3] She has been sick in the hospital.
3. Maybe [1] we should give [3] her a big helium balloon.
4. [3] They will have some ideas for [1] us at the gift store.
5. [1] We asked [3] him for some advice.
6. [3] His was the responsibility for finding the right present.
7. When [2] you saw it, [3] we could tell [1] [2] you were disappointed.
8. [3] It was a bunch of fake purple flowers.
9. [1] I didn't like [3] them at all.
10. [1] We all thought [3] they were gaudy.
11. [2] You decided [3] it was up to [1] me to find something better.
12. But the present would still be from all of [1] us.
13. [1] I picked out a pink chenille robe.
14. My friends agreed [3] hers should be pink.
15. [1] We gave [3] it to [3] her with a nice card.

B. Write **M** above the personal pronouns that refer to males, **F** above the pronouns that refer to females, and **T** above the pronouns that refer to things.

1. [F] She thanked and hugged [M] him.
2. Then [F] she tried [T] it on.
3. [M] He thought [T] it looked good on [F] her.
4. [F] She was smiling when [M] he left [F] her that day.
5. [M] He was happy that [F] she liked [T] it.

23

Name _____

23. Pronouns as Subjects

> A pronoun may be used as the subject of a sentence.
> The subject pronouns are *I, you, he, she, it, we,* and *they.*
>
> ### They laughed until tears were streaming down their faces.

A. Circle the subject pronoun in each sentence.

1. (I) just read a book about Mathew Brady.
2. (You) must have heard of him.
3. (He) was born in Warren County, New York, in 1823.
4. At 16 (he) moved to New York City to study painting.
5. (I) was surprised at his young age.
6. Soon (he) started to learn photography.
7. (It) had just been introduced in the United States.
8. In 1849 (he) opened a studio in Washington, D.C.
9. (He) began taking photos of famous people.
10. (They) all liked his wonderful pictures.

B. Change the *italicized* word(s) in each sentence to a subject pronoun. Write the pronoun on the line. Use a capital letter if necessary.

___[It]___ 1. *The Civil War* began in 1861.

___[They]___ 2. *Brady and a group of photographers* took pictures of the battlefields.

___[He]___ 3. *Brady* shocked the world by exhibiting the photos.

___[they]___ 4. For the first time *ordinary people* saw the horror of war.

___[he]___ 5. Later in his life *Brady* fell on hard times.

___[It]___ 6. *Congress* bought his negatives for $25,000.

___[She]___ 7. *My mother* is a big fan of Brady's pictures.

___[We]___ 8. *My family and I* went to an exhibition of his photographs.

___[They]___ 9. *These pictures* are the best known photographs of the Civil War.

___[It]___ 10. *His work* gives us a visual sense of days gone by.

Mathew Brady was always trying to improve his work. Give an example of how you could improve something in your life (a hobby, a project, a friendship, or some schoolwork).

24

Name _____

24. Pronouns as Subject Complements

A pronoun can replace a noun used as a subject complement. A subject complement follows a linking verb and refers to the same person, place, or thing as the subject of the sentence.

> **The winner of the award was John.**
> **The winner of the award was he.**

A. Circle the correct pronoun. Rewrite each sentence to show the subject complement as the subject. The first one is done for you.

1. The creators of the spectacle were ((they) them).
   They were the creators of the spectacle.

2. The actress who got sick was (her (she)).
   [She was the actress who got sick.]

3. The understudy who filled in was ((she) her).
   [She was the understudy who filled in.]

4. The author of the scripts was (him (he)).
   [He was the author of the scripts.]

5. The orchestra members were (them (they)).
   [They were the orchestra members.]

6. The observers of the events were ((we) us).
   [We were the observers of the events.]

7. The talented costume designer was ((he) him).
   [He was the talented costume designer.]

8. The critics who panned the show were (them (they)).
   [They were the critics who panned the show.]

9. The ushers for the show were ((they) them).
   [They were the ushers for the show.]

10. Was the ticket seller ((she) her)?
    [Was she the ticket seller?]

B. Complete each sentence with a subject pronoun. Vary your choices.

1. The confident film director was __[he]__ .
2. Is that cheerful makeup artist __[she]__ ?
3. The most talented actors are __[they]__ .
4. The worried producer is __[you]__ .
5. The new camera operators are __[we]__ .

[Possible answers are given.]

25

25. More Pronouns as Subject Complements

A subject complement follows a linking verb and refers to the same person, place, or thing as the subject of a sentence. A subject pronoun can be used as a subject complement.

A. Underline the subject complement(s) in each sentence.
Write on the line a pronoun to take the place of the noun(s).

_[he]_ 1. That boy is <u>Brian</u>.

[he, she] 2. The observer from the Boston Ballet Company is a <u>recruiter</u>.

[she] 3. The dancing teacher in the studio is <u>Ms. Lane</u>.

[they] 4. The advanced dancers are <u>Brian</u>, <u>Ling</u>, and <u>Molly</u>.

_[he]_ 5. The piano player is <u>Victor</u>.

_[he]_ 6. The man observing is <u>Mr. Blanc</u>, a retired dance teacher.

_[he]_ 7. Is that <u>Anthony</u> warming up?

[she] 8. The best dancer is <u>Molly</u>.

[they] 9. The newest dancers are <u>Marie</u> and <u>Caroline</u>.

[she] 10. It was <u>Marie</u> who could do the most pirouettes.

B. Complete each sentence with the pronoun specified.

1. Was that __[she]__? *(third, singular, female)*

2. No, it was __[he]__. *(third, singular, male)*

3. The farmer was __[she]__. *(third, singular, female)*

4. The best farmhands were __[they]__. *(third, plural)*

5. The person on the tractor is __[I]__. *(first, singular)*

6. Who is planting beans? It is __[you]__. *(second, singular)*

7. The keepers of the chickens were __[we]__. *(first, plural)*

8. Was it __[you]__ who fed the pigs? *(second, singular)*

9. Yes, it was __[I]__. *(first, singular)*

10. The farmhand in the overalls is __[he]__. *(third, singular, male)*

26. Pronouns as Direct Objects

> A pronoun may be used as the direct object of a verb.
> The object pronouns are *me, you, him, her, it, us,* and *them.*
>
> **The president chose <u>them</u> to be cabinet members.**

A. Write on the line an object pronoun to take the place of the *italicized* word(s) in each sentence.

<u>[them]</u>   1. At the Soapbox Derby I saw *motorless cars.*

<u>[it]</u>   2. Two friends built *a small wooden box with wheels and a fin.*

<u>[him]</u>   3. Katrina helped *Will* with the design.

<u>[it]</u>   4. Uncle Sharkey examined *the model* daily.

<u>[them]</u>   5. Aunt Dot encouraged *Will and Katrina.*

<u>[it]</u>   6. Finally the two friends finished *the project.*

<u>[him]</u>   7. At the race the officials registered *Will.*

<u>[them]</u>   8. The fin on the car puzzled *the judges.*

<u>[it]</u>   9. During the race the car with the fin held *the lead.*

<u>[it]</u>   10. Victoriously the soapbox crossed *the finish line.*

B. Complete each sentence with an object pronoun. [Possible answers are given.]

1. Will thanked ___[her]___ for helping with the design.

2. The audience applauded ___[them]___ as they received the grand trophy.

3. They held ___[it]___ high in the air.

4. The reporters wanted ___[them]___ to say a few words.

5. Uncle Sharkey treated ___[them]___ to lunch after the race.

C. Underline the object pronoun in each sentence.

1. Proudly Will carried <u>it</u> home.

2. The neighbors met <u>them</u> there.

3. Aunt Dot praised <u>them</u> for their work.

4. She wanted <u>them</u> to pose for pictures with the car.

5. A strong wind pushed <u>it</u> to fame.

Name _____

27. Pronouns as Objects of Prepositions

Pronouns

> An object pronoun may be used as the object of a preposition.
> **The carefully wrapped present was for <u>her</u>.**

Circle the preposition in each sentence. Write on the line the object pronoun that can take the place of the *italicized* words.

___[them]___ 1. Today the spotlight would be (on) *Joe Chapin and his classmates.*

___[him]___ 2. The teacher looked approvingly (at) *Joe.*

___[him]___ 3. (For) *Joe Chapin* class picture day was exciting!

___[them]___ 4. The photographer gave directions (to) *the students.*

___[it]___ 5. Then Mr. Ansel looked (into) *the lens.*

___[them]___ 6. Next he glanced (at) *the flowering trees.*

___[them]___ 7. The location (near) *the trees* was perfect!

___[it]___ 8. The class moved (across) *the lawn.*

___[them]___ 9. Again the photographer looked (at) *the boys and girls.*

___[her]___ 10. Joe stood (behind) *the shortest girl.*

___[her]___ 11. Mr. Ansel motioned (toward) *the last girl.*

___[it]___ 12. Then he looked (at) *the sky.*

___[them]___ 13. Rain fell (from) *some clouds.*

___[it]___ 14. We crowded (under) *a shelter nearby.*

___[it]___ 15. Mr. Ansel placed a plastic sheet (over) *his camera.*

28

28. Pronouns as Indirect Objects

An object pronoun may be used as the **indirect object** of a sentence. The indirect object tells *to whom, for whom, to what,* or *for what* the action is done. The indirect object comes between the verb and the direct object.

VERB	INDIRECT OBJECT	DIRECT OBJECT
The baker <u>sold</u>	<u>her</u>	a <u>cake</u>.

A. Circle the pronoun used as an indirect object. The direct object is *italicized*.

1. The children were bored, so Mrs. Edgars read (them) a *story*.

2. When she had finished, Carol gave (her) a *suggestion*.

3. Let's write (them) a *show*.

4. We can make (them) *costumes*.

5. They can sing (us) *songs*.

6. Please promise (me) some *help*.

7. Mrs. Edgars lent (her) a *song book*.

8. Billy was a good athlete, so she taught (him) some acrobatic *tricks*.

9. Maya was a good actress, so they assigned (her) a *role*.

10. If the neighbors want to come, we'll sell (them) *tickets*.

B. Rewrite each sentence. Use a pronoun as the indirect object.

1. The Good Witch showed Dorothy the Yellow Brick Road.
   [The Good Witch showed her the Yellow Brick Road.]

2. Dorothy brought the Tin Man the oil can.
   [Dorothy brought him the oil can.]

3. The Wicked Witch denied the travelers any help.
   [The Wicked Witch denied them any help.]

4. The Wizard promised the Scarecrow a brain.
   [The Wizard promised him a brain.]

5. The Wizard showed his visitors a diploma.
   [The Wizard showed them a diploma.]

6. The Tin Man asked the Wizard a question.
   [The Tin Man asked him a question.]

7. The Wizard granted the Tin Man a heart.
   [The Wizard granted him a heart.]

8. The Lion told the Wizard his wish.
   [The Lion told him his wish.]

9. Dorothy gave the Witch a splash of water.
   [Dorothy gave her a splash of water.]

10. The Good Witch gave Dorothy the directions home.
    [The Good Witch gave her the directions home.]

29. Subject and Object Pronouns—Part I

Pronouns

> *I* and *we* are subject pronouns.
> *Me* and *us* are object pronouns.

A. Complete each sentence with the pronoun *I* or *me*.

1. __[I]__ raked the leaves into a pile.

2. Give __[me]__ the rake.

3. That was __[I]__ in the pile of leaves.

4. __[I]__ put the leaves in garbage bags.

5. __[I]__ have finished the yard work.

6. A little dog chased __[me]__ across the yard.

7. __[I]__ like the sight of colored leaves in the fall.

8. Dad will take __[me]__ to the forest preserve to see the red and gold trees.

9. __[I]__ will find pretty leaves and press them in a book.

10. Will you give __[me]__ a paper bag for my collection of leaves?

B. Complete each sentence with the pronoun *we* or *us*.

1. __[We]__ scattered popcorn for the birds.

2. Joe saved some for __[us]__ .

3. Did the squirrels see __[us]__ ?

4. __[We]__ must be sure they don't get the popcorn before the birds do.

5. What's the matter with __[us]__ ?

6. It's not up to __[us]__ who gets the food.

7. __[We]__ should let whatever is hungry eat it.

8. Joe, will you give __[us]__ some popcorn now?

9. It is __[we]__ who should not have the popcorn.

10. Those two big bowls of it are too much for __[us]__ .

Name _____

30. Subject and Object Pronouns—Part II

> *He, she,* and *they* are subject pronouns.
> *Him, her,* and *them* are object pronouns.

A. Circle the correct pronoun in parentheses.

1. (They Them) are the men and women working on the car.

2. A wrench hit (him he) on his hand.

3. Has (he him) found the problem?

4. (She Her) has given up trying.

5. All the parts puzzle (she her).

6. (She Her) prefers fixing bicycles.

7. (He Him) is a talented mechanic.

8. Mrs. Kervick will pay (them they) for their work.

9. Do you know (they them)?

10. (He Him) took his car to another shop.

B. Choose the correct pronoun to complete each sentence and write it on the line.

he, him	1. Is the youngest baby ____[he]____ ?
they, them	2. The baby followed ____[them]____ into the next room.
They, Them	3. ____[They]____ played with the baby until dinner.
she, her	4. The cook was ____[she]____ .
He, Him	5. ____[He]____ put the food on the table.
He, Him	6. ____[He]____ is the boy nearest to the milk jug.
she, her	7. Nora wants ____[her]____ to eat the carrots.
They, Them	8. ____[They]____ planned to see a movie after dinner.
he, him	9. His little brother obeyed ____[him]____ .
He, Him	10. ____[He]____ finished everything on his plate.
she, her	11. Erica told ____[her]____ about dessert.
they, them	12. Their mother asked ____[them]____ to do the dishes.
She, Her	13. ____[She]____ cleared the dishes from the table.
He, Him	14. ____[He]____ washed the dishes.
they, them	15. Their father drove ____[them]____ to the movie theater.

31. Subject and Object Pronouns—Part III

> The subject pronouns are *I, you, he, she, it, we,* and *they.*
> The object pronouns are *me, you, him, her, it, us,* and *them.*

A. Underline each personal pronoun. Write **S** on the line if the pronoun is the subject of a sentence or a subject complement. Write **O** on the line if it is a direct object or the object of a preposition. Use column 1 for the first pronoun in the sentence and column 2 for the second.

	COLUMN 1	COLUMN 2
1. He called her on the phone.	[S]	[O]
2. She told us.	[S]	[O]
3. We talked to him about the phone call.	[S]	[O]
4. The explanation from him didn't satisfy us.	[O]	[O]
5. Did he want her to come along?	[S]	[O]
6. Ask him to have lunch with me.	[O]	[O]
7. We talked about her over dinner.	[S]	[O]
8. He and I talked a lot.	[S]	[S]
9. According to him, she is the nicest girl.	[O]	[S]
10. And what does she think of him?	[S]	[O]

B. Circle the correct personal pronoun for each sentence.

1. (**We** Us) own four pets: a dog, a cat, and two mice.
2. The barking dog frightened (**me** he).
3. (Me **I**) heard the dog barking from two blocks away.
4. The one who really loves cats is (**she** her).
5. How sad that (**you** us) are allergic to cats.
6. (**She** Her) likes to play with the cat.
7. Ted put out food for (**them** they).
8. (Them **They**) scurry across the floor.
9. Have (**you** us) considered getting a pet?
10. Next week (**we** us) will feed the neighbor's rabbit.

32. Possessive Pronouns

Possessive pronouns show possession or ownership. A possessive pronoun stands alone and often takes the place of a possessive noun. The possessive pronouns are *mine, ours, yours, his, hers, its,* and *theirs.*

The blue skateboard is Cole's. **His is the blue one.**

The green ones are TJ's and Joy's. **Theirs are green.**

A. Underline the possessive pronoun in each sentence.

1. Is that calculator <u>yours</u>?

2. <u>Hers</u> is on the desk in the second aisle.

3. <u>Mine</u> is in my backpack.

4. <u>His</u> is not here.

5. Do you think we lost <u>ours</u>?

6. Didn't the teacher say we could use <u>hers</u>?

7. I never lend <u>mine</u> to anyone.

8. <u>Yours</u> is older than Vince's.

9. I think <u>hers</u> is the most expensive.

10. Now I remember where <u>ours</u> is.

B. On the line write a possessive pronoun to replace the *italicized* word(s).

_____[his]_____ 1. The leather-bound book is *Miguel's.*

_____[theirs]_____ 2. I lost my book, but I found *Gwen's and Jessica's.*

_____[his]_____ 3. My book was an early edition, but *Jeremy's* was a first edition.

_____[Hers]_____ 4. *Julia's* is the lost one.

_____[Theirs]_____ 5. *Jane's and the teacher's* are the thickest and the heaviest.

_____[his]_____ 6. Have you asked your teacher about *Jason's*?

_____[Hers]_____ 7. *Ashley's* are on the floor in the closet.

_____[hers]_____ 8. My atlas is more current than *Vanessa's.*

_____[his]_____ 9. Do you care if I highlight your book or *David's*?

_____[Theirs]_____ 10. *Tom's and Jessica's* are on that table in the corner.

33. Possessive Adjectives

A **possessive adjective** shows possession or ownership. A possessive adjective goes before a noun. The possessive adjectives are *my, your, his, her, its, our, your,* and *their.*

SINGULAR   **my necklace**   **your sandwich**   **his/her/its bowl**
PLURAL   **our footballs**   **your sweaters**   **their magazines**

A. Underline the possessive adjective(s) in each sentence.

1. Our class had its own competition.
2. Everyone kept his or her own score.
3. The events tested your silliness.
4. We paddled our skateboards with plungers.
5. I had trouble keeping my feet on the skateboard.
6. Walking a floor balance beam, Teresa kept the book on her head.
7. Ichiro made his prize-winning beard out of shaving cream.
8. Kate used aluminum foil to make her hat.
9. How high can you count with a pencil between your nose and top lip?
10. The boys were able to hold pencils behind their ears better than the girls were.

B.   Write A if the underlined word is an adjective. Write P if it is a pronoun.

__[A]__   1. Their reasons for not winning were many.
__[A]__   2. The stick and its plunger did not stay together.
__[P]__   3. Didn't they use glue on theirs?
__[P]__   4. The stick that broke was his.
__[A]__   5. Your technique was certainly good!
__[P]__   6. Denny's ears are bigger than mine.
__[P]__   7. It's not my fault that they're bigger than yours.
__[A]__   8. Her skill at ear wiggling is unmatched.
__[P]__   9. I think the silliest stunt was ours.
__[A]__   10. This was certainly our most unusual day!

Name _____

34. Intensive Pronouns, Reflexive Pronouns

> Intensive and reflexive pronouns end in *-self* or *-selves*. An **intensive pronoun** emphasizes a noun that precedes it. A **reflexive pronoun** is used as a direct object or an indirect object of a verb or as the object of a preposition.
>
> SINGULAR myself   yourself   himself   herself   itself
> PLURAL   ourselves yourselves themselves
>
> INTENSIVE She herself made a costume. (emphasis)
> REFLEXIVE She made herself a costume. (indirect object)

A. Underline the reflexive or intensive pronoun in each sentence. Write I on the line if it is intensive and R if it is reflexive.

[I] 1. At the school play I saw him myself.
[I] 2. Did you audition for the play yourself?
[I] 3. I myself have been backstage.
[I] 4. The student usher closed the doors himself.
[I] 5. The teacher herself arranged the stage lighting.
[I] 6. The empty stage itself looks very large and intimidating.
[R] 7. The girls amused themselves while waiting for the play to begin.
[R] 8. Prepare yourself for a spectacular performance.
[R] 9. Suddenly I found myself lost in the action of the play.
[R] 10. The hurt actor blamed nobody but himself for the accident.

B. Complete each sentence with a correct pronoun. On the line write R for reflexive or I for intensive.

[I] 1. The boys [themselves] wanted to cut the birthday cake.
[I] 2. Tina [herself] made the cake from scratch.
[R] 3. You can all help [yourselves] to some ice cream.
[R] 4. They helped [themselves] to the cake.
[I] 5. The cake [itself] was covered with pink frosting and flowers.
[R] 6. The guests exhausted [themselves] by singing for the birthday girl.
[R] 7. I laughed at [myself] for being so giddy.
[I] 8. We [ourselves] helped clean up after the party.
[I] 9. Mike the Magician [himself] entertained the guests.
[I] 10. What present did you [yourself] bring, Katy?

35

35. Antecedents

> The word to which a pronoun refers is its **antecedent**. The pronoun must agree with its antecedent in number and in whether it refers to a male, a female, or a thing.
>
> ANTECEDENT PRONOUN
> **Dolley Madison was born in South Carolina, but she grew up in Pennsylvania.**

A. Circle the pronoun for the *italicized* antecedent.

1. Dolley Payne married *John Todd, Jr.,* in 1790, but (he) died three years later.

2. The young *widow* was charming, and James Madison was attracted to (her).

3. *James* and *Dolley* were of different religions, but (they) married in 1794.

4. *Dolley* was a Quaker, but (she) chose a fashionable dress for the wedding.

5. Dolley's *son* lived with the couple, and James was patient with (him).

B. Circle the antecedent for the *italicized* pronoun.

1. (James Madison) was a member of Congress; in 1801 *he* became Secretary of State.

2. (James) moved into the White House with Dolley when the people elected *him* president.

3. (Dolley) assisted at the White House whenever James asked *her* to.

4. (Diplomats) came from all over the world, and Dolley welcomed *them*.

5. Dolley fled (the White House) when the British set *it* on fire.

C. Complete each sentence with a pronoun. The antecedent is *italicized*.

1. *James* wrote to Dolley that the enemy was greater than ____[he]____ thought.

2. He said that *troops* were coming and that she should escape from ___[them]___ .

3. Dolley was determined to save official *papers,* so she stuffed ___[them]___ into trunks.

4. A *portrait* of George Washington was precious, but ____[it]____ was fastened to the wall with screws.

5. *Dolley* had the frame broken so that ____[she]____ could save the famous painting.

6. She gave the picture to two *gentlemen* and asked ___[them]___ to take it to New York.

7. *Dolley* and *James* met outside Washington, and ____[they]____ watched the city burn.

8. Years later Dolley moved with *James* to his plantation after ____[he]____ retired.

9. After James died, *Dolley* moved back to Washington, where friends helped ___[her]___ .

10. By the time *Dolley* died in 1849, ____[she]____ was beloved by all.

Name _____

36. Pronouns and Contractions

A **contraction** is made by joining two words. A contraction has an apostrophe. The apostrophe replaces one or more letters. Personal pronouns can be joined with some verbs to form contractions.

I am	I'm	we have	we've
you are	you're	he will	he'll
she is	she's	they will	they'll

A. Change each set of words in parentheses to a contraction. Write the contraction on the line. Use a capital letter when necessary.

1. (I am) __[I'm]__ reading about Boys' Festival Day in Japan.

2. On that day (they will) __[they'll]__ try to fly a 1,600-pound kite.

3. (It is) __[It's]__ an event everyone is looking forward to.

4. (They will) __[They'll]__ paint a fish on the kite.

5. (I have) __[I've]__ learned that the fish is a symbol of courage.

6. (We are) __[We're]__ going to have a kite-flying day at our school.

7. Mrs. Kelly says (she is) __[she's]__ a great kite flyer.

8. (We will) __[We'll]__ see how high her kite goes.

9. (You are) __[You're]__ going to fly your kite, aren't you?

10. (It will) __[It'll]__ be a lot of fun.

B. Circle the correct word to complete each sentence.

1. The students are going to use (they're, _their_) math, art, and science skills.

2. (_They're_, Their) going to make kites.

3. Mrs. Kelly said that (you're, _your_) kite looks beautiful.

4. I hope (_you're_, your) not going to fly that work of art!

5. (_It's_, Its) exciting to fly a kite.

6. You hold the kite up by (it's, _its_) tail.

7. (Your, _You're_) going to run as fast as you can.

8. The students took (they're, _their_) kites outside.

9. (_They're_, their) running across the field.

10. Don't let (it's, _its_) string get caught in a tree!

37. Demonstrative Pronouns, Interrogative Pronouns

Demonstrative pronouns are used to point out people, places, or things.

	SINGULAR	PLURAL
NEAR	**this**	**these**
FAR	**that**	**those**

Interrogative pronouns are used to ask questions.

<u>Who</u> owns this bike?   <u>Whom</u> did you teach to ride?

<u>Whose</u> is this skateboard?   <u>What</u> is the best skate park in town?

A. Circle the demonstrative pronoun in each sentence.
Tell whether it is singular or plural.

_____[singular]_____ 1. (This) is my favorite recipe.

_____[plural]_____ 2. (These) are the ingredients we need.

_____[singular]_____ 3. I'll put the batter in (this).

_____[singular]_____ 4. (That) is the spoon I'll use.

_____[plural]_____ 5. Please hand (those) to me.

B. Complete each sentence with a demonstrative pronoun.
Follow the directions in parentheses.

1. ___[This]___ is my old soccer uniform. *(singular, near)*

2. ___[Those]___ are my old shoes. *(plural, far)*

3. I can't wear ___[these]___ now. *(plural, near)*

4. ___[That]___ has been in my closet for months. *(singular, far)*

5. I think I'll give ___[these]___ to charity. *(plural, near)*

C. Circle the correct interrogative pronoun to complete each sentence.

1. ((Who) Whom) was Martha Dandridge Custis?

2. (Who (Whom)) did she marry?

3. ((What) Whose) was her husband George Washington like?

4. (Who (Whose)) was the house they lived in?

5. ((Who) Whose) called her a wonderful character?

6. ((Who) Whose) was called away from his wife by battles?

7. (Whose (What)) was their home called?

8. ((What) Who) did Martha write in her letters?

9. To (who (whom)) did they say goodbye?

10. ((Who) Whom) burned George Washington's papers after he died?

Name _____

38. Reviewing Pronouns

A. On the line write **1** if the *italicized* pronoun is the speaker, **2** if it is the person spoken to, or **3** if it is the person spoken about.

__[1]__ 1. Clara Barton said, "*We* need wagons for the medical supplies."

__[1]__ 2. "*We* don't have horses for the wagons," the Secretary of War told her.

__[2]__ 3. "*You* can't allow the men to be without these things," she said.

__[3]__ 4. "*They* need medical supplies badly."

__[2]__ 5. "*You* are a brave woman," he told her.

__[1]__ 6. "Mr. Stanton, allow *me* to go to the battlefield," she replied.

__[1]__ 7. "That is the place where *I* am needed most."

__[3]__ 8. She added that the wounded required attention before *they* were moved.

__[3]__ 9. "Nursing *them* on the battlefield is necessary," Miss Barton insisted.

__[2]__ 10. "*You* could get hurt if fighting were to erupt," the Secretary replied.

B. Circle the reflexive or intensive pronoun in each sentence. Write **R** on the line if the pronoun is reflexive and **I** if it is intensive.

__[I]__ 11. She ⟨herself⟩ was called the Angel of the Battlefield.

__[R]__ 12. "Clara, prepare ⟨yourself⟩ for the worst," the officers warned.

__[R]__ 13. The men helped ⟨themselves⟩ the best they could.

__[I]__ 14. I ⟨myself⟩ could never do what Clara did.

__[I]__ 15. The work ⟨itself⟩ was difficult, but Clara was determined.

C. On the line write **S** if the *italicized* pronoun is the subject. Write **SC** if it is the subject complement.

__[SC]__ 16. Our swimming teacher is *she*.

__[S]__ 17. *She* taught my brother Christopher.

__[SC]__ 18. The lifeguard is *he*.

__[S]__ 19. At the pool *he* got his swimming badge.

__[S]__ 20. *He* takes his responsibility seriously.

CONTINUED

Pronouns

D. Write the correct pronoun on the line.

I, me   21. One day Mrs. Perez asked __[me]__ to read to the class.

She, Her   22. __[She]__ handed me the book.

We, Us   23. __[We]__ were reading Harry Truman's biography.

He, Him   24. __[He]__ had many responsibilities as a child.

they, them   25. Harry did his best with each of __[them]__.

E. Write on the line a possessive pronoun for the *italicized* words in each sentence.

____[his]____ 26. My family's home is in Missouri, near *Harry Truman's*.

____[theirs]____ 27. My great grandparents' farm was next to *the Trumans'*.

____[theirs]____ 28. Unlike *most people's*, Mr. Truman's middle name was a letter.

____[his]____ 29. In my report about historic homes, *James Madison's* came first.

____[Hers]____ 30. *Barbara Jordan's* may become a tourist destination.

F. Write the contraction on the line.

31. we will   __[we'll]__   34. he is   __[he's]__

32. you have   __[you've]__   35. they are   __[they're]__

33. it will   __[it'll]__

Try It Yourself

Write four sentences about a memorable character you have
known or read about. Be sure you use pronouns correctly.

_____

_____

_____

_____

Check Your Own Work

Choose a selection from your writing portfolio, your journal, a work in progress,
an assignment from another class, or a letter. Revise it, applying the skills you have
reviewed. This checklist below will help you.

✔ Do your pronouns reflect the correct number and person?

✔ Did you use subject, object, and possessive pronouns correctly?

✔ Have you placed an apostrophe in each contraction?

39. Descriptive Adjectives

> **Adjectives** describe nouns or pronouns. Descriptive adjectives tell about the size, shape, color, weight, or other qualities of the things they describe. Some adjectives come before nouns.
>
> **courageous** firefighters   **messy** bedroom   **wonderful** aroma

A. Underline the descriptive adjectives in each sentence. The number in parentheses tells how many adjectives are in each sentence.

1. The early, golden sun shone on Sadako. (2)

2. It gave her dark hair brown highlights. (2)

3. She looked up at the clear sky. (1)

4. It was a good sign. (1)

5. Sadako went inside the small, neat house. (2)

6. She saw that her big brother was still asleep. (1)

7. "Get up, lazy one!" she said. (1)

8. The smell of delicious food filled the air. (1)

9. Hot eggs and crunchy toast awaited them in the kitchen. (2)

10. Sadako's sleepy brother dragged himself out of the comfortable bed. (2)

B. Complete each sentence with an adjective. **[Possible answers are given.]**

atomic	terrible	warm	crisp	Japanese
delicate	younger	soft	little	plain
awful	fresh	front	memorable	back

1. (Helpful) Sadako dressed her ___[younger]___ brother Eiji.

2. She put the ___[warm]___ blankets into the (large) closet.

3. In the kitchen her mother sliced ___[fresh]___ radishes.

4. This was a ___[memorable]___ day in Japan, August 6.

5. An ___[atomic]___ bomb fell on Hiroshima on this date in 1945.

6. Each year the ___[Japanese]___ people remember those who died on that (sad) day.

7. Sadako's father came in from the ___[back]___ porch.

8. He called for everyone to gather near the ___[little]___ altar.

9. A (small) picture of an (older) woman was nearby in a ___[delicate]___ frame.

10. Sadako's great grandmother had died on that ___[terrible]___ day.

C. In addition to the adjectives that you have written on the lines, there are five other adjectives in the sentences in Part B. Circle them.

40. Proper Adjectives

Some descriptive adjectives come from proper nouns and are called **proper adjectives**. Proper adjectives begin with a capital letter.

PROPER NOUN   **Mexico   Sweden**

PROPER ADJECTIVE   **Mexican   Swedish**

A. **Underline the proper adjective(s) in each sentence.**

1. Ancient Olympic games were religious festivals.

2. Roman soldiers changed the festivals to contests.

3. The games disappeared from Western culture for 1,500 years.

4. A group of German archaeologists found stadium ruins in 1875.

5. A French educator organized the modern competition.

6. The Greek people hosted the first modern games.

7. The Winter Games have often been hosted by a European nation.

8. The first medal won by a woman went to a British woman in 1900.

9. Talented athletes from Scandinavian nations compete in winter sports.

10. American athletes make us proud in winter and summer competitions.

B. **Complete each sentence with the adjective formed from the proper noun at the left.**

America 1. The ___[American]___ diver scored a perfect 10.

Poland 2. The ___[Polish]___ runner finished the marathon in record time.

Russia 3. Dancing her way to fame, the ___[Russian]___ skater performed beautifully.

Cuba 4. The ___[Cuban]___ players scored the winning point.

France 5. The ___[French]___ cyclists pedaled to the top of the velodrome.

Italy 6. One of the ___[Italian]___ relay runners dropped the baton.

Ireland 7. The ___[Irish]___ long-distance runner trained in America.

Egypt 8. In the floor exercise the ___[Egyptian]___ gymnast performed to modern music.

China 9. Despite the falling snow the ___[Chinese]___ ski jumper outdistanced everyone.

Canada 10. The ___[Canadian]___ basketball team lost by only one point.

Adjectives

41. Articles

> *A, an,* and *the* are **articles**. *A* and *an* are **indefinite articles**. An indefinite article refers to any one of a class of things. *A* is used before words beginning with a consonant sound. *An* is used before words beginning with a vowel sound.
>
> **She ate a banana.**
> **An elephant eats enormous amounts of food.**
>
> *The* is the **definite article**. It refers to one or more specific things.
>
> **She ate the banana that was in the bowl.**
> **The elephants at the sanctuary eat tons of food each day.**

Underline the definite and indefinite articles below.

Father Damien was born in the town of Tremeloo, Belgium, on the third of January, 1840. His name then was Joseph de Vesteur. Joseph went to school at a college in Braine-le-Comte. He decided to become a priest and entered an order called the Fathers of the Sacred Heart of Jesus and Mary. At this time he took the name Damien.

Damien was given the assignment of doing mission work in Hawaii. Damien took on the job with great passion. He worked with the natives of the Hawaiian Islands, and he built a number of chapels with his own hands. He is best known for being a missionary to people with Hansen's disease, or leprosy, in the settlement on the island of Molokai. This work showed great courage because leprosy is a contagious disease. Damien ministered to the people, who had no doctors or nurses to care for them. He did this in the ways he could, by helping them build houses, by dressing their sores, by comforting them, and even by digging their graves. Father Damien ministered to these sick people until he himself contracted leprosy and died.

Father Damien helped people who had no one else to take care of them. Think of a person who needs care and attention. Give an example of how you can help that person.

Name _____

42. Repetition of Articles

When two or more nouns joined by *and* name different people, places, or things, use an article before each noun. When two or more nouns joined by *and* refer to the same person, place, or thing, use an article before the first noun only.

The art teacher and the math teacher are in the gym. (more than one person)
The English teacher and drama coach is setting up the stage. (one person)

A. If the italicized phrase refers to one person, write **1**. If it refers to more than one person, write **+**.

_[+]_ 1. *A composer and a lyricist* wrote the fifth-grade show.

_[+]_ 2. *The producer and the director* selected the cast.

_[1]_ 3. *The costume designer and set decorator* made everything look great.

_[+]_ 4. *The singer, the actress, and the dancer* practiced every day.

_[1]_ 5. *The actor and comedian* was late for rehearsal.

B. For each pair of sentences, read the first sentence to determine the article(s) needed in the second sentence. If no article is needed, put an **X** on the line.
[Some answers may vary.]

1. Two people built the set. _[The]_ set designer and _[the]_ carpenter worked on it over the weekend.

2. One student did the publicity. _[The]_ writer and _[X]_ illustrator made posters.

3. One teacher provided props. _[The]_ science teacher and _[X]_ baseball coach lent bats and gloves to the cast.

4. Several students played instruments. _[The]_ lead guitarist, _[the]_ bass player, and _[the]_ drummer rehearsed in the music room.

5. One person helped the actors. _[The]_ makeup artist and _[X]_ hairstylist helped the performers get ready.

C. Complete the paragraph with articles. If no article is needed, put an **X** on the line. More than one article can be used in some cases. **[Possible answers are shown.]**

[The] musical *Wicked* is _[the]_ story of _[the]_ good witch,
1.   2.   3.
Galinda, and _[the]_ wicked witch, Elphaba. _[The]_ composer and
4.   5.
_[X]_ lyricist, Stephen Schwartz, and _[the]_ writer, Winnie Holzman,
6.   7.
tell how _[the]_ girls meet and become roommates at Shiz University.
8.
[The] pretty Galinda and _[the]_ green-skinned Elphaba are enemies
9.   10.
who become best friends. _[The]_ villain is Madame Morrible, _[the, a]_
11.   12.
sorcery teacher and _[X]_ press secretary to the Wizard. What really
13.
happened when Dorothy was blown to Oz by _[the, a]_ tornado? _[The]_
14.   15.
answer this musical gives may surprise you!

43. Demonstrative Adjectives

The **demonstrative adjectives** are *this, that, these,* and *those.*
This and *that* point out one person, place, or thing.

   this skater   **that** judge

These and *those* point out more than one person, place, or thing.

   these skaters   **those** judges

This and *these* name persons, places, or things that are near.

   this costume next to me   **these** skates in my hand

That and *those* name persons, places, or things that are far.

   that costume in the closet   **those** skates on the shelf

A. Circle the correct demonstrative adjective in parentheses.

1. In pair skating (this **these**) two compete regularly.
2. (**That** Those) skating outfit is a beautiful color.
3. The sequins on (that **those**) blouses glitter in the lights.
4. Having matching outfits makes (**that** those) pair look stylish.
5. (**This** These) pair of skates matches the sequined outfit perfectly.
6. For jumps on the ice, (**these** this) skates have toe picks.
7. (**That** Those) couple does ice dancing.
8. In their routine (that **those**) skaters can't do lifts.
9. Fast-moving music keeps (this **these**) two skating quickly.
10. (**This** These) type of skating looks like ballroom dancing.

B. Complete each sentence with the correct demonstrative adjective.

1. Figure skaters use ____[this]____ (*near*) type of skate.
2. ____[These]____ (*near*) skates have teeth cut in the front of the blade.
3. Spins and figures are made with ____[these]____ (*near*) toe picks.
4. Also, the bottoms of ____[these]____ (*near*) skates are curved.
5. ____[That]____ (*far*) skate is used just for speed skating.
6. ____[Those]____ (*far*) skate boots are inexpensive and lightweight.
7. Steel tubing reinforces ____[those]____ (*far*) thin, flat blades.
8. The blades and boots on ____[those]____ (*far*) skates are designed for speed.
9. ____[These]____ (*near*) ice-hockey skates have very heavy boots.
10. Players get support and protection from ____[that]____ (*far*) shoe.

45

Name _____

44. Adjectives That Tell How Many

Some adjectives tell how many or about how many.

SINGULAR

10th inning	either man	six games	most exams
each athlete	little time	all mice	few boxes
neither boy	much popcorn	both knees	many smiles
every girl	any child	some days	any efforts
another runner		several movies	

PLURAL

A. Underline the adjectives that tell how many. Do not include articles.

1. The pentathlon is a competition of <u>five</u> events.

2. The events are held in <u>one</u> day.

3. The <u>first</u> event is the long jump.

4. Throwing the javelin is the <u>second</u> test.

5. Before throwing the javelin, the athlete takes <u>several</u> steps.

6. <u>Each</u> athlete must also throw a discus.

7. A discus is a round metal or wooden object weighing <u>four</u> pounds.

8. An athlete holds it in <u>one</u> hand and spins around before releasing it.

9. A decathlon has <u>10</u> events.

10. It is held over a period of <u>two</u> days.

B. Complete each sentence with an adjective that tells how many.
Do not include articles. [**Possible answers are given.**]

1. The Winter Olympics are held every __[four]__ years.

2. A gold medal is the __[first]__ prize.

3. The __[second]__ prize is a silver medal.

4. A bronze medal is given as a __[third]__ prize.

5. There are __[five]__ rings on the Olympic flag.

6. __[Many]__ countries have representative athletes.

7. __[Most]__ athletes are proud just to be there.

8. __[All]__ members of teams receive individual medals.

9. __[Every]__ country should be proud of its athletes.

10. __[All]__ athletes and coaches march in the parade.

Adjectives

46

45. Position of Adjectives

An adjective usually comes before the noun it modifies.

delicate flower   **shiny** penny

When an adjective follows a linking verb, it is a subject complement. It completes the meaning of the verb and describes the subject of the sentence.

The flower is <u>delicate</u>.   **The penny was <u>shiny</u>.**

A. Underline the descriptive adjectives.

1. A <u>thick</u> mitt helps the catcher.

2. <u>Thinner</u> gloves are used by the fielders.

3. The <u>strong</u> mask protects the face of the catcher.

4. The outfielder runs carefully on the <u>wet</u> grass.

5. The gloves are made from <u>genuine</u> leather.

B. Underline the subject complement in each sentence.

1. The catcher's mitt is <u>thick</u>.

2. Fielders' gloves are <u>thinner</u>.

3. The catcher's mask is <u>strong</u>.

4. The grass is <u>wet</u>.

5. The leather in baseball gloves is <u>genuine</u>.

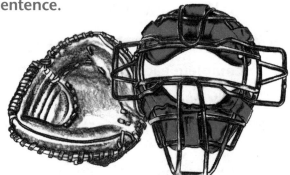

C. Underline the adjectives that come before nouns.
Circle the subject complements.

1. The <u>old</u> baseball was ⟨dirty⟩ and ⟨worn.⟩

2. The thread around the <u>corky</u> center is ⟨blue⟩ and ⟨gray.⟩

3. Under the thread the <u>black</u> and <u>red</u> material is ⟨rubbery.⟩

4. The <u>leathery</u> cover is ⟨smooth.⟩

5. The <u>precious</u> signature on it is ⟨blurry.⟩

46. Adjectives That Compare

The **positive** degree of an adjective shows a quality of a noun. The **comparative** degree is used to compare two items or two sets of items. It is often used with *than*. Many comparatives are formed by adding *-r* or *-er* to the positive. The **superlative** degree is used to compare three or more items. Many superlatives are formed by adding *-st* or *-est* to the positive. *Good* and *bad* have irregular forms of comparison.

POSITIVE	COMPARATIVE	SUPERLATIVE
Tom is tall.	Tom is taller than Jim.	Tom is the tallest boy.
Joe is thin.	Joe is thinner than Tom.	Joe is the thinnest boy.
Jim was happy.	Jim was happier than Joe.	Jim was the happiest boy.
Tom is a bad runner.	Jim is a worse runner.	Joe is the worst runner of all.

A. Write **P** if the phrase is positive, **C** if it is comparative, or **S** if it is superlative.

1. __[S]__ loudest yell

2. __[P]__ hard jab

3. __[S]__ latest class

4. __[P]__ tiny child

5. __[S]__ fastest runner

6. __[C]__ higher kick

7. __[P]__ wise choice

8. __[S]__ smoothest move

9. __[C]__ whiter robe

10. __[C]__ quicker punch

B. Complete each sentence with the adjective in the correct degree of comparison.

1. early *(superlative)*   Karate is one of the __[earliest]__ forms of unarmed combat.

2. close *(superlative)*   "Empty hand" is the __[closest]__ translation for the Japanese *kara te*.

3. fast *(comparative)*   Kung fu, Chinese karate, is __[faster]__ than karate and uses circular motions.

4. strong *(comparative)*   Tae kwon do, Korean karate, uses __[stronger]__, linear movements than other forms.

5. safe *(superlative)*   The __[safest]__ use of karate is for self-defense.

6. good *(positive)*   Karate is a __[good]__ sport for children.

7. good *(comparative)*   Most karate students have __[better]__ balance and coordination than other children.

8. good *(superlative)*   Karate is one of the __[best]__ ways to build self-confidence.

9. low *(superlative)*   The color of the belt for the __[lowest]__ level in karate is white.

10. high *(superlative)*   Students at the __[highest]__ level earn black belts.

Name _____

47. More, Most and Less, Least

Most adjectives of three or more syllables and some adjectives of two syllables do not add -er or -est to form the comparative and superlative degrees. Instead, the comparative is formed by adding *more* or *less* before the positive. The superlative is formed by adding *most* or *least* before the positive.

I am intelligent.
You are more intelligent than I.
They are the most intelligent students.

They were careless.
They are less careless than you.
She is least careless of all the girls.

A. Write the comparative and superlative of each adjective. Use *more* and *most*.

1. healthful   [more healthful]   [most healthful]
2. tolerant   [more tolerant]   [most tolerant]
3. dangerous   [more dangerous]   [most dangerous]
4. beneficial   [more beneficial]   [most beneficial]
5. nutritious   [more nutritious]   [most nutritious]

B. Write the comparative and superlative of each adjective. Use *less* and *least*.

1. successful   [less successful]   [least successful]
2. confident   [less confident]   [least confident]
3. informative   [less informative]   [least informative]
4. traditional   [less traditional]   [least traditional]
5. original   [less original]   [least original]

C. Choose the correct adjective to complete each sentence.

1. Insects are the (more numerous (most numerous)) creatures on earth.
2. Some kinds of insects are ((more destructive) most destructive) than others.
3. The (more harmful (most harmful)) insects eat crops or cause disease.
4. Predators and pollinators are the (more important (most important)) beneficial insects.
5. Ladybugs eat aphids, the (more common (most common)) plant pests.
6. Ladybug larvae are ((less ferocious) least ferocious) than they look.
7. Robber flies are ((less common) least common) than beetles.
8. Robber flies are also ((more deadly) most deadly) than many other insects.
9. Insects that pollinate flowers are the (more valuable (most valuable)) insects of all.
10. Honeybees are probably (more beneficial (most beneficial)) of all insects.

49

Name _____

48. Fewer, Fewest and Less, Least

> *Fewer, fewest, less,* and *least* are used to compare things. Use *fewer* and *fewest* with plural count nouns. Use *less* and *least* with noncount nouns. Use *fewer* and *less* to compare two things or two sets of things. Use *fewest* and *least* to compare more than two things or sets of things.
>
> **COMPARATIVE**
> This recipe requires fewer carrots.
> It requires less celery too.
>
> **SUPERLATIVE**
> That recipe requires the fewest carrots.
> It also requires the least celery.

A. Use *less* or *fewer* to write a phrase with each noun. The first one is done for you.

1. corn   less corn
2. cherries   [fewer cherries]
3. beef   [less beef]
4. bananas   [fewer bananas]
5. cookies   [fewer cookies]
6. radishes   [fewer radishes]
7. milk   [less milk]
8. lemonade   [less lemonade]
9. ice cream   [less ice cream]
10. crackers   [fewer crackers]

B. Write a phrase with each noun and *least* or *fewest*. The first one is done for you.

1. children   fewest children
2. songs   [fewest songs]
3. laughter   [least laughter]
4. attention   [least attention]
5. women   [fewest women]
6. paint   [least paint]
7. music   [least music]
8. tears   [fewest tears]
9. pencils   [fewest pencils]
10. dirt   [least dirt]

C. Circle the correct word to complete each sentence.

1. Deserts get (**less** fewer) rain than other places on earth.
2. (Less **Fewer**) kinds of plants live in deserts than in places that are more temperate.
3. (Less **Fewer**) large mammals live in deserts than in other habitats.
4. There is (**less** fewer) food for them to eat in the desert.
5. There are also (less **fewer**) places for them to find shelter.
6. Hot, dry deserts get the (**least** fewest) precipitation.
7. They have the most heat and the (**least** fewest) humidity of all deserts.
8. The Atacama Desert in Chile gets the (least **fewest**) inches of rain of any desert.
9. Cold deserts have (less **fewer**) warm days than hot, dry deserts.
10. They have (less **fewer**) rainstorms and more snowfall.

Adjectives

50

49. More on *Fewer, Fewest* and *Less, Least*

> Use *fewer* and *fewest* with plural count nouns. Use *less* and *least* with noncount nouns. Remember that some nouns can be either count or noncount, depending on how they are used.
>
> **Mom prepared fewer soups this week than she did last week. She eats less soup than anyone in the family.**

A. Complete each sentence with *fewer* or *less.*

1. A healthful diet might include more whole grains and __[less]__ white bread.

2. Eat more fruits and vegetables and __[fewer]__ sugary snacks.

3. Salads with __[less]__ salad dressing can be full of flavor.

4. Drink more water and __[fewer]__ soft drinks.

5. A proper diet can result in __[less]__ body fat.

6. Popcorn can be a good snack if it is made with __[less]__ salt and butter.

7. Orange juice contains __[less]__ fiber than whole oranges.

8. Fresh vegetables fill you up with __[fewer]__ calories than many other foods.

9. Many vegetarians eat __[less]__ fat than nonvegetarians.

10. People with food allergies may have __[fewer]__ choices than other people.

B. Complete each sentence with *fewest* or *least.*

1. I have the __[fewest]__ strange eating habits of anyone in my family.

2. My mom drinks the __[least]__ milk of us all.

3. My sister eats the __[least]__ meat.

4. My dad eats the __[fewest]__ pieces of fruit each day.

5. My brother drinks the __[fewest]__ glasses of juice.

6. Aunt Jody enjoys the __[fewest]__ kinds of dessert.

7. My cousin Harry eats the __[least]__ chocolate.

8. Uncle Norm drinks the __[fewest]__ soft drinks.

9. Grandpa likes the __[fewest]__ kinds of vegetables.

10. Grandma uses the __[least]__ salt.

50. Interrogative Adjectives

An **interrogative adjective** is used in asking a question. The interrogative adjectives are *what, which,* and *whose.* An interrogative adjective comes before a noun. *What* is used for asking about people or things. *Which* is used to ask about one of two or more people or things. *Whose* asks about possession.

> **What** kinds of animals live in coral reefs?
> **Which** coral reef have you visited?
> **Whose** job is it to protect coral reefs?

A. Circle the interrogative adjective in each sentence. Underline the noun it goes with.

1. (What) <u>animals</u> live in coral reefs?

2. (Which) <u>type</u> of coral has a limestone skeleton?

3. (Which) <u>reef</u> is the largest?

4. (Whose) <u>report</u> on coral reefs was most informative?

5. (What) <u>organizations</u> are involved in saving the reefs?

6. (What) <u>habitats</u> are in danger because of overfishing?

7. (What) <u>species</u> are in danger of becoming extinct?

8. (Whose) <u>book</u> on coral reefs did you read?

9. (What) <u>action</u> can you take to save the reefs?

10. To (which) <u>politician</u> will you write a letter?

B. Complete the sentence with a correct interrogative adjective. More than one choice may be correct. **[Answers may vary.]**

1. To ___[which, what]___ group of animals do corals belong?

2. ___[What]___ types of fish have no bones, only cartilage?

3. ___[What]___ threats are there to coral reefs today?

4. ___[Whose, Which]___ diagram of a sponge is most accurate?

5. ___[What]___ sea creatures have eight arms?

6. ___[What]___ tiny organisms do whales eat?

7. ___[Whose]___ favorite fish is the angel shark?

8. ___[What]___ reptiles usually live in a reef?

9. ___[Which, Whose]___ video on turtles was most educational?

10. ___[Whose]___ turn is it to feed the fish?

Adjectives

Name _____

51. Reviewing Adjectives

A. Complete the paragraph by writing the appropriate adjectives on the lines.

spicy	juicy	fresh	crisp	creamy
flaky	cold	crunchy	hot	delicious

[Possible answers are given.]

Athletes from various countries sat together and ate a ___[delicious]___ meal.
1.

They began with a ___[crisp]___ salad and a ___[fresh]___ fruit cup with a
2.   3.

___[creamy]___ sauce. They shared ___[spicy]___ pizza slices, ___[juicy]___
4.   5.   6.

hamburgers, tacos in ___[crunchy]___ shells, and ___[hot]___ baked potatoes.
7.   8.

Picking only one of the ___[flaky]___ French pastries was difficult. The athletes
9.

seemed to drink gallons of ___[cold]___ milk. Friendships were formed during
10.

this meal.

B. Write the proper adjective for each type of food.

11. ___[Italian]___ spaghetti (Italy)

12. ___[Belgian]___ waffles (Belgium)

13. ___[French]___ pastries (France)

14. ___[Chinese]___ chop suey (China)

15. ___[German]___ potato salad (Germany)

16. ___[Polish]___ sausage (Poland)

17. ___[Mexican]___ enchiladas (Mexico)

18. ___[Swiss]___ fondue (Switzerland)

19. ___[Japanese]___ sushi (Japan)

20. ___[Hungarian]___ goulash (Hungary)

C. Complete each sentence with the correct article.

21. __[An]__ athlete must eat a balanced diet.

22. __[A]__ balanced diet is important to his or her training.

23. Eating correctly provides your body with __[the]__ energy to compete.

24. She always eats __[a]__ piece of fruit as a snack.

25. __[The]__ fruit gives her a lot of energy.

CONTINUED

Adjectives

D. Complete each sentence with the correct demonstrative adjective (*this, that, these, those*).

26. "_[These]_ (*near*) apples look good," thought Sadako.

27. She'd like a slice of _[that]_ (*far*) watermelon.

28. Her brother wants some of _[those]_ (*far*) cherries.

29. _[This]_ (*near*) cantaloupe smells ripe.

30. _[Those]_ (*far*) grapes look delicious.

E. On the line write **P** if the *italicized* adjective is positive degree, **C** if it is comparative degree, or **S** if it is superlative degree.

_[P]_ 31. Sadako believed in signs of *good* luck.

_[P]_ 32. She looked forward to a *great* race.

_[C]_ 33. Her *older* brother encouraged her.

_[S]_ 34. He said she would be the *fastest* runner.

_[C]_ 35. Sadako knew she was *better* than she had been last year.

F. Complete each sentence with a subject complement. [Possible answers are given.]

36. Sadako was _[nervous]_ before the race.

37. Her legs were _[thin]_ but powerful.

38. When she won, Sadako was _[happy]_ .

39. Her friends were _[proud]_ of her.

40. "Sadako always was _[fast]_," said her father.

Try It Yourself

Write three sentences about your favorite meal. Be sure to use adjectives correctly.

_____

_____

_____

Check Your Own Work

Choose a selection from your writing portfolio, your journal, a work in progress, an assignment from another class, or a letter. Revise it, applying the skills you have reviewed. This checklist will help you.

✔ Have you capitalized all proper adjectives?

✔ Have you used *a* and *an* correctly?

✔ Do your demonstrative adjectives agree in number with their nouns?

✔ Have you used each adjective in the correct degree?

Adjectives

52. Action Verbs—Part I

> An **action verb** is a word used to express action.
> **Tom opened his birthday presents.**

A. Circle the action verb in each sentence.

1. Bobby (studies) every day after school.

2. Sometimes he (works) on a project with a friend.

3. Yesterday his science teacher (gave) the class an assignment.

4. Bobby (visited) his new friend John.

5. The boys (performed) the science experiment.

6. John (went) to the kitchen for a snack.

7. He (returned) with two glasses of lemonade.

8. Then the kitchen door (opened) again.

9. John (entered) with some cookies.

10. But John already (stood) beside Bobby with the lemonade!

B. Complete each sentence with an action verb. [Possible answers are given.]

1. Bobby _____[gasped]_____ in astonishment.

2. He _____[looked]_____ from one boy to the other.

3. He _____[waved]_____ his hand in front of his eyes.

4. He _____[thought]_____ he must have studied too long.

5. Sometimes your eyes _____[play]_____ tricks on you.

6. Bobby _____[jumped]_____ to his feet.

7. John _____[explained]_____ that the second boy was his twin.

8. He _____[introduced]_____ Bobby and Jason.

9. Bobby _____[laughed]_____ at their joke.

10. "You _____[fooled]_____ me!" he said.

53. Action Verbs—Part II

A. Complete each sentence with an action verb. [Possible answers are given.]

1. The Joyces ____[went]____ to the animal shelter to get a dog.

2. The puppy ____[wagged]____ its tail when it saw the children.

3. Claire ____[named]____ the dog Coco.

4. Sean ____[made]____ a bed for the puppy.

5. Sean and Claire ____[take]____ turns feeding Coco.

6. Sean ____[walks]____ the puppy after school every day.

7. Yesterday he ____[played]____ with Coco at the park.

8. There Coco ____[dug]____ a hole to bury her toy.

9. She always ____[barks]____ at strangers.

10. Coco ____[chews]____ on socks if they are on the floor.

11. Sometimes she ____[chases]____ a squirrel up a tree.

12. Coco ____[wakes]____ Claire every morning by tugging the blankets.

13. Clair ____[throws]____ Coco a ball.

14. Coco ____[catches]____ it every time!

15. At the end of the day, Coco ____[sleeps]____ in her own bed.

B. Write a sentence, using each verb. [Sentences will vary.]

giggle   1. _____

tumble   2. _____

ride   3. _____

play   4. _____

jog   5. _____

grasp   6. _____

scream   7. _____

tickle   8. _____

jump   9. _____

nap   10. _____

54. Action Verbs—Part III

A. Write an action verb that each group of people or things can perform.
[Possible answers are given.]

1. puppies _____[eat]_____   11. flowers _____[bloom]_____

2. birds _____[fly]_____   12. horses _____[gallop]_____

3. children _____[talk]_____   13. cars _____[crash]_____

4. students _____[study]_____   14. balloons _____[burst]_____

5. rock stars _____[sing]_____   15. clocks _____[tick]_____

6. authors _____[write]_____   16. tires _____[screech]_____

7. babies _____[laugh]_____   17. bunnies _____[hop]_____

8. athletes _____[jump]_____   18. fish _____[swim]_____

9. cows _____[graze]_____   19. dishes _____[break]_____

10. boats _____[float]_____   20. windows _____[shatter]_____

B. Complete each sentence with a verb from the list. Use each word once.

cried   yelled   asked   whispered   responded
called   questioned   exclaimed   shouted   replied

1. "Oh no!" _____[shouted]_____ Molly. **[Answers will vary.]**

2. "My rabbit's cage door is open, and he's gone!"

   she _____[cried]_____.

3. She _____[yelled]_____ for her sister.

4. "Have you seen Fluffy?" _____[asked]_____ Molly.

5. Hannah _____[responded]_____, "No, but I'll help you find him."

6. They _____[called]_____, "Fluffy, come here, Fluffy."

7. After looking for hours, Hannah _____[exclaimed]_____,
   "There he is, sleeping!"

8. "How sweet!" Molly _____[whispered]_____ so she wouldn't wake him.

9. "What should we do?" _____[questioned]_____ Hannah.

10. Molly _____[replied]_____, "Let's let him sleep."

Verbs

55. Being Verbs

A **being verb** is a word used to express existence. The most common being verbs are *is, are, was, were, be, been,* and *being.*

A. Circle the being verb in each sentence. If the being verb has a helping verb, circle the entire verb.

1. Traveling (is) a lot of fun.
2. I (have been) on many trips.
3. My trip to Utah (was) incredible.
4. We (were) alone in the desert under millions of stars.
5. The many stars (were) our tiny personal lanterns.
6. I (have been) to several U.S. national parks.
7. The hiking trails (will be) open soon in Grand Teton National Park.
8. The trails (were) not open last fall because of the snow.
9. It (has been) a long time since I have hiked in the mountains.
10. I hear that you (will be) in Rome soon.
11. Rome (has been) a religious site for centuries.
12. There (are) so many beautiful churches there.
13. The Vatican Museum (is) full of famous works by Michelangelo and Raphael.
14. The Sistine Chapel ceiling (has been) famous for centuries.
15. There (are) many wonderful countries, cities, and landscapes to see and explore.

B. Underline the being verbs in the paragraph.

Venice has been a major Italian city for centuries. There are few streets in Venice, but there are many canals. The biggest one is the Grand Canal. It has been the "Main Street" of Venice for a long time. The center of activity is St. Mark's Square. This is a large area near St. Mark's Cathedral. People will be there even late at night. In Venice, boats are the chief means of transportation. The gondola is a famous kind of Venetian boat. Its movement is from an oar controlled by a gondolier. Gondoliers have been the operators of these boats for centuries. Today gondolas are mainly for tourists. Boats with motors are more common now. Venice will always be an interesting and unusual city to visit.

Verbs

56. Verb Phrases

> A **verb phrase** is a group of words that does the work of a single verb.
> A verb phrase contains one or more helping verbs (*is, are, has, have, do, will, can, could, would, should,* and so on) and a main verb.
>
> Regular exercise <u>is needed</u> for good health.
> He <u>could have improved</u> his health by hiking.

Underline the verb phrase in each sentence. Write on the lines the helping verb(s) and the main verb.

	HELPING VERB	MAIN VERB
1. In the spring he <u>will hike</u> the Appalachian Trail.	[will]	[hike]
2. The Appalachian Trail is also <u>called</u> the A.T.	[is]	[called]
3. Hiking the trail from end to end <u>is called</u> thru-hiking.	[is]	[called]
4. A thru-hiker <u>will cross</u> about 2,100 miles.	[will]	[cross]
5. The trail <u>has been marked</u> with blazes.	[has been]	[marked]
6. White rectangular marks <u>have been painted</u> on trees.	[have been]	[painted]
7. Blazes <u>can keep</u> hikers from becoming lost.	[can]	[keep]
8. Hikers <u>should make</u> camp before sundown.	[should]	[make]
9. On the A.T. a camper <u>can find</u> shelters a day's hike apart.	[can]	[find]
10. Many people <u>have camped</u> along the trail.	[have]	[camped]
11. Porcupines <u>are sighted</u> near some campsites.	[are]	[sighted]
12. Black bears <u>have appeared</u> along the trail.	[have]	[appeared]
13. Campers <u>should leave</u> no trace after using a campsite.	[should]	[leave]
14. You <u>should visit</u> the A.T. once in your lifetime.	[should]	[visit]
15. Thousands of people <u>will hike</u> the trail this year.	[will]	[hike]

57. More Verb Phrases

> In questions and negative statements the helping verb and the main verb may be separated.
>
> **Will** you **come** to the party tonight?   They **are** not **expected** to be there.

A. Underline the main verb and the helping verb in each sentence.

1. <u>Do</u> you <u>like</u> dogs?
2. Carlos <u>does</u> not <u>own</u> a dog.
3. <u>Do</u> Dalmatians <u>have</u> spots?
4. <u>Has</u> Frisky <u>been</u> to the veterinarian yet?
5. Frisky <u>did</u> not <u>enjoy</u> the vaccination.
6. <u>Can</u> Great Danes <u>grow</u> that tall?
7. <u>Was</u> Frisky <u>walked</u> after school?
8. My dog <u>does</u> not <u>bark</u> often.
9. Poodles <u>do</u> not <u>shed</u> much.
10. <u>Did</u> Bandit <u>dig</u> that hole in the yard?
11. What <u>do</u> English foxhounds <u>like</u> to hunt?
12. <u>Can</u> your dog <u>jump</u> over the fence?
13. <u>Do</u> you <u>brush</u> your Old English sheepdog often in the summer?
14. <u>Can</u> your Saint Bernard <u>fit</u> through the door?
15. <u>Were</u> chows <u>used</u> for hunting?

B. Answer each question with a negative response. Underline the main verb and the helping verb in the question and the response. **[Possible answers are given.]**

1. <u>Did</u> you <u>watch</u> the late movie last night?
   [I did not watch the late movie last night.]
   _____

2. <u>May</u> she <u>go</u> to the movies tonight?
   [She may not go to the movies tonight.]
   _____

3. <u>Should</u> we <u>watch</u> the film at nine o'clock?
   [We should not watch the film at nine o'clock.]
   _____

4. <u>Will</u> he <u>buy</u> popcorn for the show?
   [He will not buy popcorn for the show.]
   _____

5. <u>Are</u> they <u>paying</u> for the show themselves?
   [They are not paying for the show themselves.]
   _____

58. Principal Parts of Verbs

A verb has four **principal parts: present, present participle, past,** and **past participle.** The present participle of verbs is formed by adding *-ing* to the present part. For verbs ending in *e,* drop the final *e* before adding *-ing.* The present participle is used with forms of the helping verb *be (am, is, are, was, were, been).*

> jump   jumping   scrape   scraping   tap   tapping

The past and the past participle of regular verbs is formed by adding *-d* or *-ed* to the present part. For verbs ending in *y* following a consonant, change the *y* to *i* before adding *-ed.* The past participle is used with the helping verb *have (has, had).*

> jump   jumped   scrape   scraped   fry   fried

For single-syllable verbs that end with a consonant following a vowel, double the final consonant before adding *-ing* or *-ed.*

> step   stepping   stepped

A. Write the present participle, the past, and the past participle of each verb.

	PRESENT PARTICIPLE	PAST	PAST PARTICIPLE
1. cheer	[cheering]	[cheered]	[cheered]
2. sigh	[sighing]	[sighed]	[sighed]
3. play	[playing]	[played]	[played]
4. laugh	[laughing]	[laughed]	[laughed]
5. walk	[walking]	[walked]	[walked]
6. roll	[rolling]	[rolled]	[rolled]
7. yell	[yelling]	[yelled]	[yelled]
8. sneeze	[sneezing]	[sneezed]	[sneezed]
9. hop	[hopping]	[hopped]	[hopped]
10. crawl	[crawling]	[crawled]	[crawled]

B. Write a sentence, using the direction in parentheses and the verb *jump.*

1. (Use the past tense.)   [Sentences will vary.] _____

2. (Use the present tense.)   _____

3. (Use the present participle.) _____

4. (Use the past tense.)   _____

5. (Use the past participle.)   _____

59. Regular and Irregular Verbs

> The past and past participle of regular verbs end in *-ed* or *-d.*
> The past and past participles of **irregular verbs** do not end in -ed or -d.

A. Underline the verb or verb phrase in each sentence. Write **R** on the line if the principal verb is regular or **I** if it is irregular.

___[I]___ 1. Recently our class took a trip to the Vietnam War Memorial.

___[R]___ 2. The memorial is located in Washington, D.C.

___[I]___ 3. It was built in honor of those who served in Vietnam.

___[R]___ 4. The names of all the dead were carved in stone.

___[R]___ 5. Family members and friends have often visited the memorial.

___[I]___ 6. Some found the name of deceased loved ones.

___[I]___ 7. Often they left flowers at the site.

___[I]___ 8. The flowers were a sign of remembrance.

___[I]___ 9. The memorial has made a lasting impression on each visitor.

___[R]___ 10. We have learned to appreciate the sacrifices of those who served.

B. Write a sentence, using each verb in the past tense. Write **R** on the line if the verb is regular or **I** if it is irregular. [Sentences will vary.]

___[I]___ 1. buy _____

___[I]___ 2. eat _____

___[R]___ 3. laugh _____

___[R]___ 4. walk _____

___[R]___ 5. study _____

___[I]___ 6. make _____

___[R]___ 7. answer _____

___[I]___ 8. know _____

___[R]___ 9. paint _____

___[R]___ 10. talk _____

Verbs

60. More Regular and Irregular Verbs

A. Complete each sentence with the simple past or the past participle of the verb. Remember to use the past participle if the sentence has a helping verb.

fall 1. How much rain _____[fell]_____ here last year?

study 2. Scientists have _____[studied]_____ rainfall for years.

collect 3. The rain is _____[collected]_____ in a bucket.

stop 4. When the rain has _____[stopped]_____, the scientists measure the depth.

make 5. They have _____[made]_____ studies of the weather cycle from the results.

be 6. Rain has always _____[been]_____ an important source of fresh water.

cause 7. Today air pollutants have _____[caused]_____ some rainwater to be unhealthful.

result 8. Many human activities have also _____[resulted]_____ in polluted water.

find 9. Polluted water has been _____[found]_____ to be dangerous to human health.

learn 10. We _____[learned]_____ that polluted water can make us sick.

B. Complete each sentence with the simple past or the past participle of the verb.

eat 1. Mike had _____[eaten]_____ his breakfast early that day.

grow 2. The plant _____[grew]_____ two inches.

give 3. I had _____[given]_____ my catcher's mitt to my friend.

go 4. Who _____[went]_____ to the game yesterday?

throw 5. The outfielder _____[threw]_____ the ball to the catcher.

teach 6. Our teacher had _____[taught]_____ us how to add fractions.

display 7. Harold _____[displayed]_____ the population data in a circle graph.

try 8. We _____[tried]_____ that solution to the equation.

jump 9. The athlete _____[jumped]_____ rope for exercise.

stand 10. Fans _____[stood]_____ in line for concert tickets.

Verbs

63

61. Am, Is, Are, Was, and Were

> The present tense forms of the verb *be* are *am, is,* and *are.* The past tense forms are *was* and *were.* Use *am* with the first person singular pronoun *I.* Use *is* or *was* with a singular noun or the third person singular pronoun *he, she,* or *it.* Use *are* or *were* with a plural noun, the first person plural pronoun *we,* the second person pronoun *you,* or the third person plural pronoun *they.*
>
> I am glad to be here.   I was here yesterday.
> You are a talented musician.   You were not here yet.
> The musicians in the band are great.   The musicians were on stage.

A. Circle the correct form of *be* in parentheses.

1. Minerals and vitamins (is **are**) some of the body's essential nutrients.

2. Some minerals (is **are**) present in the body in tiny, or trace, amounts.

3. Calcium (**is** are) important for the growth of bones.

4. Vitamins (is **are**) thought to promote health.

5. Vegetables (is **are**) good sources of vitamins.

B. Complete each sentence with *am, is,* or *are.*

1. Your friends __[are]__ here.

2. What __[is]__ the matter?

3. I __[am]__ on the phone.

4. She __[is]__ ready to go.

5. __[Are]__ you sure you want to leave now?

C. Circle the correct form of *be* in parentheses.

1. (**Was** Were) Jeff in the science lab with you?

2. He (**was** were) not in the lab yesterday.

3. The teacher (**was** were) quite helpful.

4. The students (was **were**) disappointed with the result.

5. The final exam (**was** were) difficult.

D. Complete each sentence with *was* or *were.*

1. The children __[were]__ surprised.

2. The clowns __[were]__ on tiny bikes.

3. The magician __[was]__ in black.

4. The rabbit __[was]__ in the magician's hat.

5. __[Were]__ you at the circus too?

Verbs

62. Do, Does, Doesn't, and Don't

> Use *does* or *doesn't* (*does not*) when the subject is a singular noun or a third person singular subject pronoun (*he, she, it*).
>
> **The striped shirt <u>does</u> go with that plain skirt.**
> **He <u>doesn't</u> seem to have a lunch.**
>
> Use *do* or *don't* (*do not*) when the subject is a plural noun or with the subject pronouns *I, we, you,* and *they.*
>
> **Motorists <u>do</u> like clearly marked street signs.**
> **We <u>don't</u> have the money to go on vacation right now.**

Verbs

A. Circle the correct verb in parentheses.

1. This chair (**does** do) match the other chairs.

2. (**Doesn't** Don't) this striped velvet look good on it?

3. I (doesn't **don't**) usually like that material.

4. The couch (**does** do) look comfortable.

5. (Doesn't **Don't**) you like sitting on leather?

6. I (does **do**) like sitting on things that are soft.

7. Velvet (**doesn't** don't) look so bad to me now.

8. Why (doesn't **don't**) we try covering the couch with it?

9. (**Does** do) it cost a fortune?

10. Yes, because we (doesn't **don't**) get it wholesale.

B. Complete each sentence with *does* or *doesn't* or *do* or *don't.*

1. Those curtains ____[do, don't]____ hang gracefully.

2. ____[Do, Don't]____ they have ties to hold them back?

3. One tie ____[does, doesn't]____ work.

4. ____[Does, Doesn't]____ the living room look nice when the curtains are drawn?

5. The sun and the breeze ____[do, don't]____ come in when the curtains are closed.

6. The room ____[does, doesn't]____ look gloomy now.

7. ____[Do, Don't]____ you think the room could use more color?

8. ____[Does, Doesn't]____ that yellow pillow cheer things up?

9. One pillow ____[does, doesn't]____ make the couch more comfortable.

10. ____[Do, Don't]____ you want to buy some bright fabrics for this room?

63. Come and Go, Bring and Take

> The verb *come* means "to move toward something." Its principal parts are *come, coming, came,* and *come.* The verb *go* means "to move away from a place." Its principal parts are *go, going, went,* and *gone.*
>
> **He <u>came</u> into the room with an armful of books.**
> **Later he <u>went</u> out the side door to the gym.**
>
> The verb *bring* denotes action toward the speaker. Its principal parts are *bring, bringing, brought,* and *brought.* The verb *take* indicates an action toward another place. Its principal parts are *take, taking, took,* and *taken.*
>
> **<u>Bring</u> your math book to my house this evening.**
> **You may <u>take</u> my camera on your field trip to the museum.**

A. Circle the correct verb in parentheses.

1. Will you (**take** bring) this letter to the post office, please?

2. When you return, (take **bring**) some batteries from the hardware store.

3. Lou (took **brought**) his flashlight to my house, but the batteries were dead.

4. I wish he had (taken **brought**) me a flashlight with good batteries.

5. Will he be (**taking** bringing) the equipment to the gym tomorrow?

B. Circle the correct verb in parentheses.

1. Phil (comes **goes**) to that restaurant regularly.

2. You can see from across the street how many people (come **go**) into the restaurant.

3. My aunt plans to visit that restaurant when she (**comes** goes) to town to visit us.

4. I wish she would (**come** go) to visit soon because I enjoy her company.

5. After she has (come **gone**) to see all her other nephews, she will stop by our house.

C. Write one sentence each, using the present participle of *take, bring, come,* and *go.* Then write one sentence, using *take* in the past tense.

1. [Sentences will vary.] _____

2. _____

3. _____

4. _____

5. _____

Verbs

64. Sit and Set, Teach and Learn

> The verb *sit (sitting, sat, sat)* means "to have a place" or "to keep a seat."
> The verb *set (setting, set, set)* means "to place" or "to fix in position."
>
> **He sat there all day, staring into the distance.**
> **She set the clock on her nightstand and set it for five a.m.**
>
> The verb *teach (teaching, taught, taught)* means "to give instruction" or "to pass on knowledge." The verb *learn (learning, learned, learned)* means "to receive instruction or knowledge."
>
> **Ana teaches history to fifth graders.**
> **The children have learned a lot about the colonists.**

A. Circle the correct verb in parentheses.

1. We (sit (set)) the trophy on the top shelf.

2. I ((sit) set) across from my sister at the dinner table.

3. The dog (set (sat)) on the steps all morning.

4. My brother ((sits) sets) too close to the TV.

5. I (sat (set)) the glass next to the knife.

B. Complete each sentence with a correct form of *sit* or *set*.

1. Who __[sat]__ on the porch swing yesterday?

2. __[Sit]__ here and rest for a while.

3. Where should I __[set]__ the table?

4. Please __[set]__ the table for dinner.

5. The baby __[sits]__ in her high chair.

C. Circle the correct verb in parentheses.

1. My grandfather ((taught) learned) me how to cook.

2. I (taught (learned)) to make meatloaf first.

3. Anyone who ((teaches) learns) someone must be patient.

4. My mother (taught (learned)) that I like to taste as I cook.

5. She ((taught) learned) me that cooking is an art.

D. Complete each sentence with a correct form of *teach* or *learn*.

1. Last year in school we __[learned]__ about sound.

2. This year we __[are learning]__ about volcanoes.

3. Our math teacher last year __[taught]__ us how to divide.

4. Some students __[learned, learn]__ long division very slowly.

5. I wish someone had __[taught]__ me French!

65. Simple Tenses

The **tense of a verb** shows the time of its action. There are three simple tenses. The **simple present tense** tells about something that is always true or about an action that happens again and again. The **simple past tense** tells about an action that happened in the past. The **future tense** tells about an action that will happen.

SIMPLE PRESENT   **The children <u>play</u> games at recess.**

SIMPLE PAST   **They <u>played</u> quietly for an hour.**

FUTURE   **They <u>are going to play</u> softball tomorrow.**

          They <u>will leave</u> early.

Verbs

Underline the verb or verb phrase in each sentence. Write the tense on the line.

___[present]___ 1. Years after her death, Dorothea Dix still <u>lives</u> in history books.

___[past]___ 2. Dorothea <u>spent</u> much of her life in Maine and Massachusetts.

___[past]___ 3. She <u>carried</u> the heartache of an unhappy childhood.

___[present]___ 4. Dorothea <u>presents</u> an image of a teacher in the early 1800s.

___[past]___ 5. At age 14 she <u>founded</u> a school for young children.

___[past]___ 6. Dorothea <u>learned</u> of the problems of people with mental illness.

___[past]___ 7. She <u>devoted</u> her life to their care.

___[present]___ 8. People with mental illness still <u>need</u> help today.

___[future]___ 9. Where <u>are</u> they <u>going to find</u> this help?

___[past]___ 10. She <u>investigated</u> jails' treatment of the mentally ill.

___[past]___ 11. With a rich friend's help, Dorothea <u>built</u> a state hospital in New Jersey.

___[past]___ 12. In Europe she <u>educated</u> nurses on patient care.

___[future]___ 13. Because of Dorothea, nurses <u>will continue</u> the study of all aspects of patient care.

___[present]___ 14. Only a very generous person <u>volunteers</u> to serve others.

___[present]___ 15. Dorothea's epitaph <u>describes</u> her as the most useful and distinguished woman in America.

Dorothea Dix believed in helping people with physical and mental illnesses, so she fought for their rights. How can you serve others? Give an example.

66. Subject-Verb Agreement

A subject and a verb always agree in number and person. If the subject is a third person singular noun or *he, she,* or *it,* add *-s* or *-es* to the end of the verb. Noncount nouns are always considered singular.

> **I eat breakfast every day.**   **The bus waits at the red light.**
> **You wait for the bus at six o'clock.**   **She eats lunch in the cafeteria.**
>   **The cat watches the mouse.**

Plural nouns and the subject pronouns *we, you,* and *they* must always have verbs that do not add *-s* or *-es.*

> **Bikers observe traffic laws.**
> **They carry their lunches with them.**
> **We buy the same newspaper every day.**

Verbs

Circle the correct verb form in parentheses. The subject is *italicized.*

1. Each year my *father* (visit (visits)) my grandparents in Ireland.

2. *He* (stay (stays)) two weeks each time.

3. *He* (take (takes)) along pictures of my brothers and me.

4. My *grandfather* ((is) are) always surprised by how much we've grown.

5. My *grandparents* ((take) takes) my father to see relatives.

6. *They* (has (have)) tea and sandwiches.

7. The *tea* ((is) are) made with milk and sugar.

8. My *grandmother* (know (knows)) many old Irish songs.

9. *She* ((is) are) always singing them.

10. My *grandparents* (has (have)) a dog named Shep.

11. My *grandfather* (walk (walks)) to the shore every morning.

12. *People* (is (are)) at work catching lobsters.

13. *Shep* (go (goes)) with my grandfather.

14. A *donkey* ((is) are) in their backyard.

15. My *father* always (bring (brings)) gifts from my grandparents.

Name _____

67. Progressive Tenses

The **present progressive tense** tells what is happening now. The present progressive tense is formed with a present form of the verb *be (am, is, are)* and the present participle.

He **is riding** his bike in the park.

The **past progressive tense** tells what was happening in the past. The past progressive tense is formed with a past form of the verb *be (was, were)* and the present participle.

He **was riding** his bike when the accident happened.

The **future progressive tense** tells what will be happening in the future. The future progressive tense is formed with *will, is going to,* or *are going to* with *be* and the present participle.

He **is going to be having** a cast put on his ankle.

Underline the verb phrase in each sentence.
Write the tense on the line.

1. We <u>are</u> all <u>having</u> a great day. [present progressive]

2. The sun <u>is shining</u>. [present progressive]

3. Later we <u>will be playing</u> kick ball. [future progressive]

4. It <u>was raining</u> a while ago. [past progressive]

5. Trees <u>were swaying</u> in the strong wind. [past progressive]

6. Now I <u>am strolling</u> through the park. [present progressive]

7. Children <u>are playing</u> on the swings. [present progressive]

8. People <u>are eating</u> their lunches in the sunshine. [present progressive]

9. In the fall the sun <u>will be setting</u> much earlier. [future progressive]

10. Now everyone <u>is enjoying</u> the nice weather. [present progressive]

11. Yesterday at this time I <u>was sitting</u> in school. [past progressive]

12. The teacher <u>was explaining</u> the movements of planets. [past progressive]

13. They <u>are</u> all <u>revolving</u> around the sun. [present progressive]

14. They <u>are</u> also <u>rotating</u> on their axes. [present progressive]

15. Next week we <u>will be studying</u> cloud types. [future progressive]

70

68. Present Perfect Tense

The **present perfect tense** tells about an action that happened at some indefinite time in the past or an action that started in the past and continues into the present time. The present perfect tense is formed with *have* or *has* and the past participle.

Alma <u>has made</u> potato salad for the reunion.

A. Underline the present perfect tense verb in each sentence.

1. My mother's family <u>has had</u> a family reunion every summer for years.

2. My family <u>has gone</u> to the reunion since I was a baby.

3. We <u>have enjoyed</u> ourselves every time.

4. For the last five years the reunions <u>have been</u> at the local park.

5. Cousin Ona <u>has won</u> the sack race more times than I can count.

6. For years my uncles <u>have been</u> in charge of the grill.

7. Now the cousins <u>have announced</u> that they want to take over the job.

8. My grandmother <u>has outdone</u> herself this year.

9. She <u>has made</u> three piñatas!

10. We <u>have</u> already <u>started</u> the plans for next year's reunion.

B. Complete each sentence with the present perfect tense of the verb.

ask   1. Many eager fans __[have asked]__ the star for her autograph.

try   2. She __[has tried]__ to avoid them.

refuse   3. She __[has refused]__ to leave her hotel room.

gather   4. Hundreds of people __[have gathered]__ on the sidewalk.

wait   5. They __[have waited]__ patiently for hours.

make   6. Many of them __[have made]__ signs with her name.

speak   7. Her manager __[has spoken]__ to her several times.

urge   8. He __[has urged]__ her to wave from the window.

arrive   9. A limousine __[has arrived]__ to take her to the awards ceremony.

tell   10. The driver __[has told]__ the fans to leave.

69. Past Perfect Tense

> The **past perfect tense** tells about a past action that was completed before another past action started. The past perfect tense is formed with *had* and the past participle.
>
> **Seth had eaten three slices of ham before his mother got home.**

A. Underline the past perfect tense verb in each sentence.

1. In the 1800s scientists claimed they <u>had found</u> canals on Mars.
2. They said that space creatures <u>had dug</u> the canals.
3. People believed that life <u>had existed</u> on that planet.
4. The scientists <u>had seen</u> channels but not canals dug by living creatures.
5. The channels might prove that water <u>had been</u> there at some time in the past.
6. Long before humans sent out spacecraft, writers <u>had imagined</u> life on Mars.
7. By the 1890s H. G. Wells <u>had written</u> about an invasion of Earth by Martians.
8. Ray Bradbury's book *The Martian Chronicles* said that inhabitants of Earth <u>had invaded</u> Mars.
9. Before the Mars Rovers landed, no one <u>had known</u> what the planet was really like.
10. Scientists <u>had created</u> Martian conditions in a lab here before they tested a rover on Mars.

B. Complete each sentence with the past perfect tense of the verb.

think
1. Before the discoveries of Galileo Galilei, most people __[had thought]__ that the sun revolved around the earth.

read
2. By the early 1600s Galileo __[had read]__ about telescopes.

make
3. Within a short time Galileo __[had made]__ his own telescope.

discover
4. After he __[had discovered]__ four of Jupiter's moons, Galileo looked at the Milky Way.

believe
5. Before Galileo learned that the Milky Way is made up of stars, scientists __[had believed]__ that it was just a cloud.

observe
6. Galileo was the first European to discover sunspots, although Chinese astronomers __[had observed]__ them much earlier.

focus
7. After he __[had focused]__ his telescope on the moon, Galileo announced that the moon had mountains and craters.

conclude
8. By 1616 Galileo __[had concluded]__ that the earth revolves around the sun.

write
9. Some officials were angry because Galileo __[had written]__ that the earth moves.

publish
10. He was brought to trial because he __[had published]__ his views.

70. Future Perfect Tense

> The **future perfect tense** is used to talk about a future event that will be started and completed before another future event. The future perfect tense is formed with *will have* and the past participle.
>
> **We <u>will have eaten</u> lunch by the time the game starts.**

A. Underline the future perfect tense verb in each sentence.

1. By next month the students <u>will have completed</u> their projects for the science fair.

2. Bill and Henry <u>will have chosen</u> their project by the end of today.

3. By Monday Carla <u>will have constructed</u> her volcano.

4. Laura and Bryan <u>will have designed</u> their rocket by the end of the week.

5. Mr. Navarro <u>will have mailed</u> the applications by Friday.

6. Before his lettuce has sprouted, Vijay <u>will have read</u> about organic fertilizers.

7. Mia <u>will have finished</u> her model of the solar system by next Thursday.

8. By next week Keith <u>will have collected</u> all the materials he needs for his project.

9. By the time she's finished, Ann <u>will have tried</u> her experiment many times.

10. Everyone <u>will have worked</u> hard to finish on time.

B. Complete each sentence with the future perfect tense of the verb.

drive   1. By the end of the week, we __[will have driven]__ across South Dakota.

reach   2. By Monday afternoon we __[will have reached]__ the city of Mitchell.

visit   3. Before dinnertime we __[will have visited]__ the Corn Palace.

cross   4. By lunchtime on Tuesday we __[will have crossed]__ the Missouri River.

drive   5. We __[will have driven]__ to the Badlands by Tuesday evening.

see   6. By Wednesday we __[will have seen]__ bison at Custer State Park.

explore   7. By Thursday night we __[will have explored]__ Jewel Cave.

stop   8. Before leaving Hot Springs, we __[will have stopped]__ at Mammoth Site.

view   9. Before heading home, we __[will have viewed]__ Mount Rushmore.

have   10. We hope that by then we __[will have had]__ a great time.

Name _____

71. Linking Verbs

A **linking verb** links, or joins, a subject with a subject complement, which identifies or describes the subject. The subject complement may be a noun, a pronoun, or an adjective. Verbs of being are linking verbs.

NOUN   She *is* the <u>teacher</u> of this class.
PRONOUN   The talented artist *was* <u>he</u>.
ADJECTIVE   The man behind the counter *was* <u>gruff</u>.

Verbs

A. Circle the subject complement in each sentence. Write on the line whether it is a noun, a pronoun, or an adjective. The linking verbs are *italicized*.

_____[noun]_____ 1. The orange *is* a (fruit) that contains vitamin C.

_____[adjective]_____ 2. Those apples *are* (green.)

_____[pronoun]_____ 3. The fruit vendor *was* (he.)

_____[noun]_____ 4. Honeydew *is* the (melon) my mother likes least.

_____[adjective]_____ 5. The rotten bananas *were* (mushy.)

_____[noun]_____ 6. These strawberries and blueberries *are* our (dessert) tonight.

_____[noun]_____ 7. Peaches *are* the main (ingredient) in this pie.

_____[pronoun]_____ 8. The best fruit-smoothie maker *is* (she.)

_____[noun]_____ 9. Those fresh apples *will be* (cobbler) when she is finished with them.

_____[adjective]_____ 10. The pie-making contest *has* always *been* (fun.)

B. Complete each sentence with a subject complement. Use a noun, a pronoun, or an adjective. [**Answers will vary.**]

1. The Art Institute of Chicago is a _____ that millions of people visit every year.

2. Monet and Picasso are _____ whose works hang in the Art Institute.

3. Water lilies have been the _____ of some of Monet's greatest paintings.

4. The water lilies are _____.

5. Was it not _____ who purchased the painting for a million dollars?

74

Name _____

72. Reviewing Verbs

A. Underline the verb in each sentence. Circle **A** if it is an action verb or **B** if it is a being verb.

1. We <u>walked</u> along the beach. (A) B
2. The sun <u>was</u> warm. A (B)
3. Waves <u>lapped</u> against the shore. (A) B
4. A seagull <u>soared</u> overhead. (A) B
5. We <u>were</u> happy to be there. A (B)

B. Underline the verb phrase in each sentence. Write the helping verb on the line.

___[had]___ 6. Marie <u>had run</u> along the beach earlier.

___[Did]___ 7. <u>Did</u> she <u>pass</u> the hot dog stand?

___[will]___ 8. She <u>will buy</u> a salad for lunch.

___[might]___ 9. We <u>might have</u> salad for lunch too.

___[can]___ 10. We <u>can decide</u> that later.

C. Write the principal parts of each verb.

	PRESENT PARTICIPLE	PAST	PAST PARTICIPLE
11. break	[breaking]	[broke]	[broken]
12. call	[calling]	[called]	[called]
13. make	[making]	[made]	[made]
14. choose	[choosing]	[chose]	[chosen]
15. go	[going]	[went]	[gone]

D. Circle the correct verb in parentheses.

16. (Bring (Take)) the map with you when you leave.

17. Friends at the party said Myrna had left and had ((gone) come) home.

18. Will you ((bring) take) refreshments when you come here for the meeting?

19. I (brought (took)) the audio equipment from the storeroom over to the gym.

20. When Kyle (comes (goes)) on the next field trip, he should wear sunglasses.

E. Circle the linking verb or verb phrase. Underline the subject complement and write **N** if it is a noun, **A** if it is an adjective, or **P** if it is a pronoun.

21. The boys (are) almost <u>identical</u>. ___[A]___

22. Perhaps the first boy (was) <u>John</u>. ___[N]___

23. The second boy (looks) <u>taller</u>. ___[A]___

24. I think the second boy (is) <u>he</u>. ___[P]___

25. The first boy (could be) <u>his cousin</u>. ___[N]___

CONTINUED

Name _____

F. What is the tense of the underlined verb in each sentence? Write *present, past, future, present progressive, past progressive, future progressive, present perfect, past perfect,* or *future perfect* on the line. Not all tenses are used.

_____[present]_____ 26. Pelicans <u>live</u> on every continent except Antarctica.

_____[present perfect]_____ 27. Scientists <u>have found</u> pelican fossils almost 40 million years old.

_____[past perfect]_____ 28. I <u>had</u> often <u>watched</u> pelicans on trips to the beach.

_____[past]_____ 29. A soaring brown pelican <u>spied</u> a fish far below in the water.

_____[past progressive]_____ 30. Seconds later the bird <u>was plunging</u> rapidly toward its prey.

_____[past]_____ 31. The bird <u>scooped</u> the fish into its large beak.

_____[present]_____ 32. Pelicans <u>live</u> very long lives.

_____[past perfect]_____ 33. Scientists found one bird that they <u>had banded</u> more than 30 years earlier.

_____[future]_____ 34. <u>Will</u> these birds <u>become</u> extinct?

_____[future progressive]_____ 35. I hope I <u>will be watching</u> pelicans for a long time.

Try It Yourself
Write four sentences about something funny or amazing that happened to you. Be sure to use verbs correctly.

_____

_____

_____

_____

Check Your Own Work
Choose a selection from your writing portfolio, your journal, a work in progress, an assignment from another class, or a letter. Revise it, applying the skills you have reviewed. This checklist will help you.

✔ Have you used the correct forms of irregular verbs?

✔ Have you used the correct tenses?

✔ Do your subjects agree with your verbs in person and number?

Verbs

76

Name _____

73. Adverbs of Time

> An **adverb** modifies a verb, an adjective, or another adverb.
>
> **He ran <u>swiftly</u>.** (modifies verb *ran*)
> **She is <u>extremely</u> intelligent.** (modifies adjective *intelligent*)
> **My father spoke <u>quite</u> sternly to me.** (modifies adverb *sternly*)
>
> **Adverbs of time** answer the question *when* or *how often.* Some adverbs of time are *again, already, always, before, early, finally, frequently, now, often, soon, today,* and *yesterday.*

A. Underline the adverb in each sentence that tells *when* or *how often.*

1. Miriam told me a story <u>yesterday</u>.

2. I had not heard it <u>before</u>.

3. <u>Today</u> she promised to tell me two more.

4. <u>First</u> an African tale will be presented.

5. Who knows what will happen <u>next</u>!

6. <u>Once</u> there lived a very poor couple.

7. They were <u>usually</u> dressed in rags.

8. They had no children, but they <u>often</u> wished for some.

9. They <u>always</u> hoped for a better future.

10. <u>Sometimes</u> they dreamed about what might happen.

B. Circle the adverb of time in each sentence and write it on the line.

_____[once]_____ 1. The poor man (once) met a man named Abinuku.

_____[soon]_____ 2. They (soon) became friends.

_____[seldom]_____ 3. Abinuku was (seldom) happy or content.

_____[usually]_____ 4. He (usually) held much hate in his heart.

_____[seldom]_____ 5. The poor man (seldom) knew Abinuku's true feelings.

_____[frequently]_____ 6. The poor man (frequently) prayed for a better life.

_____[finally]_____ 7. Help was (finally) promised to him.

_____[Often]_____ 8. (Often) Money, Child, and Patience would visit him.

_____[then]_____ 9. He would (then) have to choose which gift to keep.

_____[ever]_____ 10. How could he (ever) choose?

74. Adverbs of Place

> **Adverbs of place** answer the question *where.*
>
> ## The farmer fell <u>backward</u> into the haystack.
> (Where did the farmer fall? He fell *backward.*)
>
> Some adverbs of place are *above, away, backward, below, down, forth, here, in, out, there,* and *up.*

A. Underline the adverb in each sentence that tells *where.*

1. We stood <u>there</u> on the busiest corner.

2. My mother shops <u>here</u>.

3. We looked <u>upward</u> to the top of the new mall.

4. Someone decided it was time to go <u>forward</u> and shop.

5. I would go <u>in</u> if I had money.

6. She took the escalator <u>down</u> to the floor with the shoe stores.

7. The salesperson walked <u>away</u> from the counter.

8. My mother's friend walked <u>on</u> as we tried a new computer.

9. They all met <u>inside</u> to have lunch.

10. I walked <u>ahead</u> toward the movie theater.

B. Complete each sentence with an adverb of place. **[Possible answers are given.]**

1. You will find the athletes _____[inside]_____, near the locker room.

2. They won't come _____[out]_____ before they stretch.

3. Their fans gather _____[everywhere]_____ at Wimbledon.

4. Tennis professionals like playing _____[here]_____.

5. Two players walk _____[down]_____ toward the court.

6. The judges come _____[forward]_____ and greet them, wishing them both luck.

7. The line judge stands _____[there]_____ to observe the line.

8. A player runs _____[up]_____ to the net.

9. The camera crew moves _____[backward]_____ when the player approaches them.

10. The winner walks _____[away]_____ from the match with a trophy and a smile.

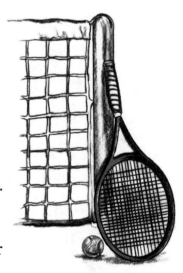

Adverbs

Name _____

75. Adverbs of Manner

> **Adverbs of manner** answer the question *how*.
>
> **The contestant spelled the word <u>correctly</u>.**
> (How did the contestant spell the word?
> The contestant spelled it *correctly*.)
>
> Some adverbs of manner are *carefully, correctly, fast, gracefully, hard, kindly, quickly, softly, swiftly, truthfully*, and *well*.

A. Underline the adverb in each sentence that tells *how* or *in what manner*.

1. The court jester danced <u>wildly</u> for the king.

2. The queen wore her crown <u>beautifully</u>.

3. The serfs worked <u>diligently</u> in the fields.

4. They suffered <u>greatly</u> from their poor living conditions.

5. The king spoke <u>distinctly</u> to his subjects.

6. Two guards stood <u>silently</u> at the castle's gate.

7. They <u>proudly</u> protected the castle.

8. The guard <u>carefully</u> aimed his bow and arrow.

9. The king's army fought <u>heroically</u> at the battle.

10. The king and queen danced <u>elegantly</u> at the ball.

B. Complete each sentence with an adverb of manner.

1. Joshua draws and paints _____[well]_____.

2. He applies the paint _____[gracefully]_____.

3. His hand draws _____[steadily]_____ on the paper.

4. No one speaks _____[loudly]_____ in his studio.

5. I go to see his art _____[eagerly]_____.

6. When I paint, I move the brush _____[slowly]_____.

7. I must go to art class _____[quickly]_____.

[Possible answers are given.]

8. In class we paint and draw _____[happily]_____.

9. Josh likes to draw when music is playing _____[softly]_____.

10. He paints _____[carefully]_____ every morning.

Name _____

76. Adverbs of Time, Place, and Manner

Underline the adverb in each sentence.
Write on the line to tell if it expresses time, place, or manner.

___[time]___ 1. In Omaha, Nebraska, Father Edward J. Flanagan <u>regularly</u> studied the plight of young boys who were orphans, delinquents, or criminals.

___[time]___ 2. He decided to work <u>daily</u> for their cause.

___[manner]___ 3. For the boys to move <u>successfully</u> through life, they needed an education.

___[time]___ 4. Father Flanagan started what is <u>now</u> the Girls and Boys Town school system.

___[manner]___ 5. He <u>earnestly</u> collected money to rent an old mansion as a home for boys.

___[place]___ 6. Father Flanagan's policy was to welcome any boy who wanted to be <u>there</u>.

___[time]___ 7. The boys played sports and <u>frequently</u> played music.

___[manner]___ 8. When the school outgrew that space, Father Flanagan <u>determinedly</u> found another.

___[place]___ 9. Father Flanagan bought a farm that was located <u>nearby</u>.

___[time]___ 10. A home could <u>finally</u> be built to accommodate all the boys.

___[manner]___ 11. On it the boys could work <u>hard</u> and produce some of their own food.

___[time]___ 12. This home would <u>soon</u> be called Boys Town.

___[place]___ 13. Girls and Boys Towns can be found <u>elsewhere</u> in our country.

___[manner]___ 14. Their workers <u>tirelessly</u> serve not only girls and boys but families as well.

___[manner]___ 15. We need people like Father Flanagan, who have faith in humanity and who give <u>generously</u> of themselves.

Adverbs (side tab)

Father Flanagan cared for boys who were outcasts of society.
He believed in them when no one else did. Give an example
of something kind you can do for someone in your class
or school who is not accepted by the crowd.

Name _____

77. Adverbs That Compare

Many adverbs have three **degrees of comparison: positive, comparative,** and **superlative.**
The comparative of most adverbs that end in *-ly* is formed by adding *more* or *less* before the positive.
The superlative is formed by adding *most* or *least* before the positive.

| quickly | more quickly | most quickly |
| sadly | less sadly | least sadly |

The comparative of most adverbs that do not end in *-ly* is formed by adding *-er.* The superlative is formed by adding *-est.*

| soon | sooner | soonest |
| far | farther | farthest |

A. Underline the adverb in each sentence. Write on the line the degree of comparison.

[positive] 1. The rooster woke us <u>early</u> in the morning.

[comparative] 2. A cheetah can run <u>faster</u> than a lion.

[superlative] 3. The brown puppy opened its eyes <u>widest</u> of all.

[comparative] 4. In the city you will see squirrels <u>more often</u> than rabbits.

[positive] 5. The old man treats his cats <u>kindly</u>.

[positive] 6. The crew worked <u>hard</u> at building the dam.

[comparative] 7. The seagull flew <u>higher</u> than the pelican.

[positive] 8. The bear cub tried <u>earnestly</u> to catch a salmon.

[comparative] 9. A snail travels <u>more slowly</u> than many other animals.

[superlative] 10. I think the gazelle runs <u>most gracefully</u> of all.

B. Circle the correct adverb in parentheses.

1. Of all the rainy days, today it is raining (harder (hardest)).
2. You must walk (carefully (more carefully)) when it is raining than when it is not.
3. We ((politely) more politely) folded our umbrellas when we entered her house.
4. The eagle flew (high (higher)) than usual to avoid the rain.
5. This is the (more awful (most awful)) weather we've had in a long time.

Adverbs

81

78. Good and Well

> The word *good* is an adjective. Adjectives modify nouns or pronouns.
> *Good* may follow a linking verb as a subject complement.
>
> **The mushroom pizza was a <u>good</u> choice.** (modifies the noun *choice*)
> **They are <u>good</u> at playing soccer.** (modifies the pronoun *they*)
>
> *Good* answers the question *what kind*.
>
> **She was a <u>good</u> babysitter.**
> (*What kind* of babysitter was she? She was a *good* one.)
>
> The word *well* is generally an adverb. Adverbs usually modify verbs.
> *Well* often modifies a verb and answers the question *how*.
>
> **Susan plays <u>well</u> with other children.**
> (*How* does she play with other children? She plays *well*.)

Adverbs

A. Circle the correct word in parentheses.

1. Andy cleaned his room (good (well)).

2. This room could use a ((good) well) dusting.

3. ((Good) Well) cleaning supplies will help a lot.

4. If we don't dry the window (good (well)), it will have streaks.

5. Lots of ((good) well) effort is what we need.

6. Did you know that newspaper dries a mirror or window (good (well))?

7. It's a ((good) well) idea to begin dusting at the top of the walls and work toward the floor.

8. If we don't do a ((good) well) job, your mother will notice.

9. He doesn't do as (good (well)) with the broom and the mop as he does with the vacuum cleaner.

10. We have worked together (good (well)) and now have an immaculate house.

B. Complete each sentence with *good* or *well*.

1. The shining sun seemed to say it was going to be a __[good]__ day.

2. For some reason I couldn't listen __[well]__ in class today.

3. I had no __[good]__ reason for misspelling that easy word.

4. The teacher explained the decimal problem __[well]__.

5. When things don't go __[well]__, I consult my older brother.

79. Real and Very

Real is an adjective and means "genuine or true."

Believe it or not, that was a <u>real</u> monkey in our yard.

Very is an adverb and means "extremely or to a high degree."

Marina was <u>very</u> cautious as she walked along the ledge.

A. Complete each sentence with *real* or *very*.

1. I am always __[very]__ happy to visit the art museum.

2. You can see many __[real]__ masterpieces there.

3. The art teachers were __[very]__ eager to see Edgar Degas's work.

4. Degas sculpted human figures __[very]__ well.

5. Degas sometimes used __[real]__ ballerinas as models.

6. He was __[very]__ interested in capturing the mood of dancers backstage.

7. The art student had a __[real]__ interest in art depicting dance.

8. The museum shop has a __[very]__ good collection of Degas prints.

9. An art collector would rather have the __[real]__ thing.

10. It was __[very]__ thoughtful of you to buy me this Degas print.

B. Circle the correct word in parentheses.

1. Brioche is a (real (very)) tasty kind of bread.

2. It is made with lots of ((real) very) butter.

3. The ((real) very) recipe calls for a special pan.

4. When I am (real (very)) hungry, a brioche and some tea are the perfect snack.

5. I am (real (very)) picky about the breads I eat.

6. They must be (real (very)) fresh.

7. Fresh bread is a gift of ((real) very) appeal for many people.

8. The crust is often (real (very)) brown and crunchy.

9. The ((real) very) test of whether a bread is good is if Grandma will eat it.

10. Thick slices of fresh bread help make a (real (very)) hearty sandwich.

Name _____

80. No, Not, Never

A negative idea is expressed by using one negative word.
This negative word may be *no, not, none, never,* or *nothing.*

> **There was <u>nothing</u> she could say to make me change my mind.**

If a sentence has one negative word, do not add another. Use a word
such as *any* or *ever* instead.

A. Circle the correct word in parentheses.

1. None of my friends has (**ever** never) seen a farm.
2. Aren't there (**any** no) farms near the city?
3. I have (ever **never**) ridden on a tractor.
4. There were (any **no**) scarecrows in the fields.
5. Didn't she gather (**any** no) eggs from the hens?
6. Isn't there (**anything** nothing) I can do for the harvest?
7. Haven't you baled (**any** no) hay?
8. There are (any **no**) farmhands on this farm at all.
9. There was (any **no**) way to save the crop.
10. She has (ever **never**) seen cattle.

B. Complete each sentence to express a negative idea.

1. Bill hasn't found ___[any]___ mail in his mailbox.
2. Have you ___[never]___ received a package by special delivery?
3. I have ___[never, not]___ been sent flowers.
4. Did you ___[not]___ bring stamps with you?
5. This package hasn't ___[any]___ postage.
6. There was ___[no]___ address on this envelope.
7. Vince has ___[never, not]___ had a pen pal.
8. You can't write if you haven't ___[any]___ stationery.
9. Haven't you ___[ever]___ received a chain letter?
10. Aren't there ___[any]___ mailboxes nearby?

Adverbs

Name _____

81. *There Is* and *There Are*

When a sentence begins with *there* followed by a form of the verb *be,* the subject of the sentence comes after the verb. *There is* or *there was* is used with a singular subject. *There are* or *there were* is used with a plural subject.

	VERB		**SUBJECT**	
There	is	a large	tree	in our backyard.
There	are		flowers	growing under the tree.

A. Underline the subject of each sentence. Write **S** if the subject is singular or **P** if the subject is plural.

[P]   1. There are several <u>parks</u> in downtown Chicago.

[P]   2. There are modern <u>sculptures</u> in Millennium Park.

[S]   3. There is a <u>sculpture</u> that looks like a huge, shiny bean.

[S]   4. There is a large <u>fountain</u> with two tall towers.

[P]   5. There are <u>pictures</u> of faces projected on the towers.

[S]   6. There is shallow <u>water</u> for children to play in.

[S]   7. There is a <u>stage</u> in the park.

[P]   8. There are <u>concerts</u> there in the summertime.

[P]   9. There are <u>restaurants</u> near the stage.

[P]   10. There are many <u>things</u> to do and see.

B. Write *was* or *were* to complete each sentence.

1. There __[was]__ a kite festival in my neighborhood last week.
2. There __[were]__ kites of every size and shape.
3. There __[were]__ free kite-making kits for children.
4. There __[was]__ an instructor who taught us how to fly kites.
5. There __[were]__ strolling musicians.
6. There __[was]__ a food cart at the edge of the field.
7. There __[was]__ a craft booth where kids made kite-shaped magnets.
8. There __[were]__ clowns walking on stilts.
9. There __[was]__ a nice breeze that day.
10. There __[were]__ dozens of kites in the sky.

Adverbs

82. Adverb Clauses

A **clause** is a group of words with a subject and a predicate. An **independent clause** expresses a complete thought and can stand on its own as a sentence. A **dependent clause** does not express a complete thought and cannot stand on its own as a sentence. An **adverb clause** is a dependent clause used as an adverb. An adverb clause often answers the question *when.* Common conjunctions used to introduce adverb clauses are *after, as, as soon as, before, once, since, until, when, whenever,* and *while.*

> **I will do my homework before we eat dinner.**
> **After I do the dishes, I'll play video games.**

Underline the adverb clause in each sentence. Look for the conjunctions for help.

1. Kit Carson's father died <u>when Kit was only nine years old</u>.

2. <u>After Kit turned fourteen</u>, he became a saddle maker.

3. <u>When Kit was nineteen</u>, he moved west and became a fur trapper.

4. <u>While he was trapping</u>, he got to know many Native Americans.

5. <u>Whenever people talked about Kit</u>, they said he was brave and honest.

6. Kit met John Frémont <u>while Kit was visiting Missouri</u>.

7. Kit guided John <u>as they traveled all over the West</u>.

8. <u>When John published his journal of the trip</u>, Kit became famous.

9. Kit led U.S. troops <u>when war broke out with Mexico in 1846</u>.

10. <u>After the war ended</u>, Kit became a rancher in the New Mexico Territory.

11. He served as a federal Indian agent for northern New Mexico <u>until the Civil War started</u>.

12. <u>When the Civil War broke out</u>, Kit helped organize New Mexico's infantry.

13. <u>Before Kit retired</u>, he moved Navajos from their land to a reservation.

14. <u>As soon as the war was over</u>, Kit left the army and went back to ranching.

15. <u>Since his death in 1868</u>, there have been books, movies, and television shows about his life.

Kit Carson had the interest and the ambition to do many different things during his life. Name some of the things you are interested in doing. Do you need courage to do them?

Name _____

83. Reviewing Adverbs

A. Write on the line whether the *italicized* adverb is an adverb of time, place, or manner.

_____[time]_____ 1. A storm hit our town *yesterday*.

_____[manner]_____ 2. The sky *quickly* got dark.

_____[time]_____ 3. *Next* the wind began to gust.

_____[place]_____ 4. Thunder cracked *overhead*.

_____[manner]_____ 5. Rain beat *loudly* against the windows.

B. Complete the chart with the comparative and superlative of each adverb.

	COMPARATIVE	SUPERLATIVE
6. fast	[faster]	[fastest]
7. faithfully	[more, less faithfully]	[most, least faithfully]
8. swiftly	[more, less swiftly]	[most, least swiftly]
9. high	[higher]	[highest]
10. far	[farther]	[farthest]

C. Write *is* or *are* to complete each sentence.

11. There _____[is]_____ a great park near my house.

12. There _____[are]_____ swings and slides for little kids.

13. There _____[are]_____ softball fields too.

14. There _____[is]_____ a pool for swimmers.

15. There _____[are]_____ activities for everyone.

D. Underline the adverb clause in each sentence. Look for the conjunctions for help.

16. <u>Before we leave for the lake</u>, we pack up the car.

17. We sing silly songs <u>while we are on the way</u>.

18. <u>As soon as we arrive</u>, we run for the water.

19. <u>When we are tired of swimming</u>, we eat lunch.

20. We hike in the woods <u>after we take a nap</u>.

Adverbs

Name _____

E. Circle the correct word in parentheses.

21. The poor man went to Abinuku for (well **good**) advice.

22. Abinuku was (**very** real) jealous of him.

23. Abinuku (ever **never**) wanted the poor man to be happy.

24. "You must choose (good **well**)," Abinuku said.

25. "(None **No**) other decision should be considered as carefully as this one."

26. "A (**good** well) choice," he said, "would be Patience."

27. Abinuku thought, "It won't bring him (no **any**) happiness."

28. The poor man wanted (**nothing** anything) but to make the right choice.

29. At first his wife was (**very** real) angry.

30. Eventually, however, Patience brought them (very **real**) joy.

31. (Nothing **None**) of the other gifts could have made them more content.

32. They couldn't remember (**ever** never) being so happy.

33. Money and Child came to the couple too, and they were (ever **never**) a problem.

34. The couple didn't need (no **any**) other gifts.

35. In the end Abinuku had advised the poor man (good **well**).

Try It Yourself

Write four sentences about a storm or other severe weather you have witnessed. Be sure to use adverbs correctly.

_____

_____

_____

_____

Check Your Own Work

Choose a selection from your writing portfolio, your journal,
a work in progress, an assignment from another class, or a letter.
Revise it, applying the skills you have reviewed.
This checklist will help you.

✔ Have you included appropriate adverbs of time, place, and manner?

✔ Have you used the correct degree of comparison for the adverbs?

✔ Have you used *good* and *well*, negative words, and *real* and *very* correctly?

Adverbs

Name _____

84. Prepositions and Their Objects

> A **preposition** is a word that shows the relationship between a noun or a pronoun and another word in the sentence. The noun or pronoun that follows the preposition is the **object of the preposition**.
>
> **Little Red Riding Hood went into the woods.**
> (*Woods* is the object of the preposition *into*.)
>
> Here are some common prepositions.
>
> | | | | | | |
> |---|---|---|---|---|---|
> | about | against | between | for | of | to |
> | above | among | by | from | off | toward |
> | across | at | down | in | on | under |
> | after | before | during | into | over | up |
> | around | beside | except | near | through | with |

A. Complete each sentence with an appropriate preposition.
[Possible answers are given.]

1. We enjoyed sledding _____[on]_____ the hill.

2. James slid _____[into]_____ a snow bank.

3. Don't fall _____[off]_____ the sled, Luchi.

4. Vince took the ski lift
   _____[up]_____ the mountain.

5. He skied _____[down]_____
   the slopes.

6. We took a sleigh ride
   _____[through]_____ the woods.

7. The ride took us _____[toward]_____
   a stream.

8. We went _____[over]_____ a snow-covered bridge.

9. Ice skate _____[with]_____ us, Anna.

10. Her skates were a gift _____[from]_____ her aunt.

B. Circle the prepositions in these sentences.

1. John Chapman was born (in) Massachusetts (in) 1775.

2. Johnny's dream was planting apple trees (for) settlers.

3. His dream could not come true (without) hard work.

4. He went (into) several orchards and collected a lot (of) seeds.

5. A law required that settlers plant 50 trees (on) their land.

Name _____

85. Prepositional Phrases

> A preposition and the noun or pronoun that follows it are separate words, but they do the work of a single modifier. This group of related words is called a phrase. Because it is introduced by a preposition, it is called a **prepositional phrase**.
>
> **Little Red Riding Hood went <u>into the woods</u>.**

A. Circle the preposition(s) and underline the prepositional phrase(s) in each sentence.

1. (At) first John Chapman gave bags (of) seeds (to) settlers.

2. Later he traveled (to) Pennsylvania.

3. (After) some time, he journeyed (to) the Ohio Valley.

4. Johnny took saplings (with) him everywhere.

5. He planted them (beside) running streams.

6. He also planted orchards (on) rolling hills.

7. He could not notice a fertile area (without) stopping.

8. Johnny moved (from) place (to) place, planting more trees.

9. (Throughout) the area he became known (as) Johnny Appleseed.

10. Thanks (to) him, the Ohio Valley is rich (in) apple trees.

B. Complete each sentence with a prepositional phrase. [Answers will vary.]

1. The gardener bent _____.

2. He planted the wildflower seeds _____.

3. He put some ladybugs _____.

4. I gave the gardener a spade, which he placed _____.

5. The gardener placed a bouquet _____.

Prepositions, Conjunctions, Interjections

86. Between and Among

Use the preposition *between* when speaking of two persons, places, or things.
   Let's keep this information between you and me.

Use the preposition *among* when speaking of more than two persons, places, or things.
   The singer stood unrecognized among her fans.

A. **Circle the correct preposition in parentheses.**

1. Amy walked (between) among) her two sisters.
2. The United States lies (between) among) the Atlantic and the Pacific oceans.
3. Distribute the papers (between (among)) the students in the class.
4. A beautiful flower grew (between (among)) the dozens of weeds.
5. The band marched (between) among) two lines of spectators.
6. The two boys carried the injured man (between) among) them.
7. Four of the Great Lakes lie (between) among) the United States and Canada.
8. Is there a secret (between) among) the two of you?
9. Our airplane is (between (among)) those three on the runway.
10. You may sit (between) among) Austin and me.
11. Alabama is (between) among) Georgia and Mississippi.
12. Good leaders work for peace (between (among)) all the nations of the world.
13. Share the fruit (between (among)) the four of you.
14. The flower arrangement sat (between) among) two candles.
15. Not one (between (among)) the students would miss the field trip.

B. **Complete each sentence with *between* or *among*.**

1. Those five boys often quarrel _____[among]_____ themselves.
2. Trade is carried on _____[between]_____ North and South America.
3. There isn't one tall player _____[among]_____ the five.
4. _____[Between]_____ you and me, whom shall we choose?
5. The awards were divided _____[among]_____ the three top winners.
6. There is a joyful spirit _____[among]_____ the students in our class.
7. The garage stands _____[between]_____ the house and the barn.
8. There was one stranger _____[among]_____ the four visitors.
9. _____[Between]_____ them, the two brothers made the model ship.
10. May I walk _____[between]_____ Ian and you?

Name _____

87. From and Off

> *From* generally refers to moving away; it indicates a starting point for a physical movement. *From* may also refer to the source of something.
>
> **We traveled from Virginia to New Jersey.**
> **The invitation was from my neighbors.**
>
> *Off* is used to indicate the removal or separation of something. The expression *off of* is never correct.
>
> CORRECT: **He took the tag off his shirt.**
> INCORRECT: **He took the tag off of his shirt.**

A. **Circle the correct preposition in parentheses.**

1. The label came (from (off)) the jar when it got wet.
2. We bought corn ((from) off) the farmer.
3. She swept the leaves (off of (off)) the porch.
4. ((From) Off) whom did you receive that interesting book?
5. Take the message ((from) off) him, please.
6. Who slid (off of (off)) the seat?
7. These skates are a gift ((from) off) my uncle.
8. The boy hopped (from (off)) his bicycle.
9. This watch is a present ((from) off) my grandparents.
10. It was hard to get the top (off of (off)) the ketchup bottle.

B. **Complete each sentence with *from* or *off*.**

1. Don't jump ___[off]___ the step.
2. We get peanuts ___[from]___ farmers.
3. The farmhand hopped ___[off]___ the tractor.
4. My mother buys spices ___[from]___ that shopkeeper.
5. I get interesting books ___[from]___ my uncle.
6. The sign read, "Keep ___[off]___ the grass."
7. The lid fell ___[off]___ the jar.
8. Kevin stepped ___[off]___ the train quickly.
9. I learned how to print ___[from]___ my teacher.
10. You may get a paper ___[from]___ the instructor.

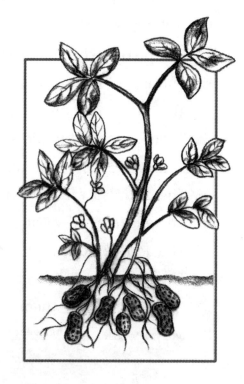

Prepositions, Conjunctions, Interjections

Name _____

88. Prepositional Phrases as Adjectives

An **adjective phrase** is a prepositional phrase used as an adjective. An adjective phrase contains a preposition and an object.
The ballerina with the pink tutu danced gracefully.

A. Underline the adjective phrase in each sentence. Identify the noun each adjective phrase modifies. Write the noun on the line.

[flowers] 1. The flowers in the vase look lovely.

[garden] 2. They are from the garden behind the house.

[roses] 3. The roses along the trellis are red, yellow, and pink.

[ivy] 4. The ivy on the house is growing quickly.

[tree] 5. The tree beside the house shades the lawn.

[daffodils] 6. The daffodils with yellow trumpets stand nearby.

[zinnias] 7. The zinnias near the trellis are very cheerful.

[shrub] 8. The shrub in the corner is fragrant and colorful.

[lilies] 9. The lilies in this garden have showy flowers.

[plant] 10. The plant with heart-shaped flowers is called a bleeding heart.

B. Read the paragraph. Underline the adjective phrases. Circle the noun each phrase modifies.

Are you a (person) with hay fever? Hay fever is an (allergy) with definite symptoms. All (seasons) except winter are bad (times) for sufferers. This allergy produces uncomfortable (irritations) in the eyes, nose, and throat. The (eyes) of the victim may become red, itchy, and watery. The (nose) with its swollen membranes may itch and run. The (throat) with its sensitivity becomes irritated. What is the (cause) of all this grief? (Pollen) from plants is the culprit! If you have (symptoms) of this annoying condition, many remedies are available.

Prepositions, Conjunctions, Interjections

93

Name _____

89. More Prepositional Phrases as Adjectives

Rewrite each sentence, changing the *italicized* adjective to an adjective phrase. **[Possible answers are given.]**

1. The *tour* guide spoke perfect English.

   [The guide of the tour spoke perfect English.]

2. She pointed out the *marble* statue.

   [She pointed out the statue of marble.]

3. Then she showed us the *Vermeer* painting.

   [Then she showed us the painting by Vermeer.]

4. The *gold* crown was behind glass.

   [The crown of gold was behind glass.]

5. We could touch the *silver* rings though.

   [We could touch the rings of silver though.]

6. A *German* tourist asked many questions.

   [A tourist from Germany asked many questions.]

7. His friends wanted to stop for some *Italian* coffee.

   [His friends wanted to stop for some coffee from Italy.]

8. We were all hoping there would be some *French* bread.

   [We were all hoping there would be some bread from France.]

9. We settled for *cheese* sandwiches.

   [We settled for sandwiches of cheese.]

10. The *tour* bus could not fit between the cars.

    [The bus for the tour could not fit between the cars.]

Prepositions, Conjunctions, Interjections

Name _____

90. Prepositional Phrases as Adverbs

> An **adverb phrase** is a prepositional phrase used as an adverb.
> An adverb phrase contains a preposition and an object.
> **The rain drove the team into the dugout.**

A. Underline the adverb phrase in each sentence.
Write on the line the verb it modifies.

_____[led]_____ 1. The tour guide's words led us <u>into the past</u>.

_____[jousted]_____ 2. She described the knights who jousted <u>outside the castle walls</u>.

_____[watched]_____ 3. The lord of the castle watched <u>from the battlements</u>.

_____[sat]_____ 4. His lady sat <u>in the tower</u>.

_____[lowered]_____ 5. The guards lowered the drawbridge <u>over the moat</u>.

_____[stood]_____ 6. When drawn, the bridge stood <u>against the gate</u>.

_____[shot]_____ 7. The guards shot arrows <u>through the loopholes in the castle walls</u>.

_____[feasted]_____ 8. All the castle's residents feasted <u>in the great hall</u>.

_____[disappeared]_____ 9. The lady disappeared <u>up the spiral staircase</u>.

_____[came]_____ 10. The feast's herbs and vegetables came <u>from the castle's small garden</u>.

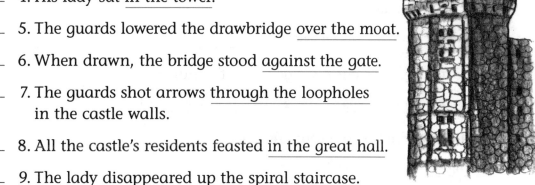

B. Complete each sentence with an adverb phrase. **[Possible answers are given.]**

1. The plane flies _____[over the ocean.]_____

2. We traveled _____[to foreign lands.]_____

3. We gave our passports _____[to the customs official.]_____

4. The guide placed our bags _____[on the cart.]_____

5. The pickpocket reached _____[into my bag.]_____

6. We bought the strange fruit _____[in the market.]_____

7. I put the train tickets _____[on the counter.]_____

8. My passport fell _____[out of the pouch.]_____

9. We misplaced the money _____[at the hotel.]_____

10. We won't travel again _____[without travelers' checks.]_____

91. More Prepositional Phrases as Adverbs

Rewrite each sentence, changing the *italicized* adverb
to an adverb phrase. [Possible answers are given.]

1. The surgeon operated *skillfully* on the patient.

   [The surgeon operated with skill on the patient.]

2. The patient lay *silently* on the operating table.

   [The patient lay in silence on the operating table.]

3. Her husband paced *worriedly* up and down the hallway.

   [Her husband paced with worry up and down the hallway.]

4. The patient recovered *speedily*.

   [The patient recovered with speed.]

5. The bandages were changed *gently* by the nurse.

   [The bandages were changed with gentleness by the nurse.]

6. The night nurse ran the unit *efficiently*.

   [The night nurse ran the unit with efficiency.]

7. The technician performed the tests *quickly*.

   [The technician performed the tests with quickness.]

8. The elderly patient moved her leg *painfully*.

   [The elderly patient moved her leg with pain.]

9. The orderly pushed the gurney *clumsily* into the elevator.

   [The orderly pushed the gurney with clumsiness into the elevator.]

10. The doctor diagnosed the problem *expertly*.

    [The doctor diagnosed the problem with expertise.]

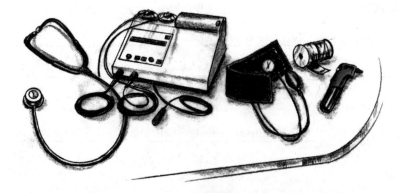

Prepositions, Conjunctions, Interjections

Name _____

92. Prepositional Phrases as Adjectives or Adverbs

Read the sentences. Circle the adjective phrases. Underline the adverb phrases.

1. The Statue of Liberty stands in New York Harbor.

2. It was erected in 1886.

3. It was a gift from France.

4. *Liberty Enlightening the World* was the name the artist gave to the statue.

5. "The New Colossus" was another name given to the statue.

6. This title comes from a poem.

7. The poem was written by Emma Lazarus.

8. She was a poet from New York City.

9. She called the statue "Mother of Exiles" in her poem.

10. The statue in the poem gives a "world-wide welcome."

11. What she wrote in her poem was heartfelt.

12. In the late 1800s America was welcoming numerous immigrants.

13. These were immigrants from many nations.

14. Emma cared particularly about the Jewish people who came here, because she herself was Jewish.

15. Her family could trace its Jewish heritage to America's early settlement.

16. Emma spoke on Jewish issues.

17. She started classes for Jewish immigrants.

18. She helped them find housing in the city.

19. She published her poem "The New Colossus" in 1883.

20. Her poem eventually was engraved on the Statue of Liberty's plaque.

Emma Lazarus tried to help people who were new to this country. Give an example of something you can do to help someone who is new to your class, school, or neighborhood.

Name _____

93. Conjunctions with Subjects

A **conjunction** is a word that connects words or groups of words.

Would you like to play volleyball <u>or</u> soccer?

The most common conjunctions are coordinating conjunctions such as *and, or,* and *but.* A **coordinating conjunction** connects words or groups of words that are of equal importance in a sentence, such as the parts of a compound subject. A sentence with two or more subjects has a **compound subject.**

<u>Women</u> <u>and</u> <u>men</u> sprinted after the dog.

A. Circle the conjunction in each sentence. Underline the subjects it connects.

1. <u>Today</u> (and) <u>tomorrow</u> will be special program days at my school.
2. The <u>students</u> (or) the <u>teachers</u> are going to sit in the front rows in the gym.
3. <u>Tracy</u> (and) <u>Trina</u> will sit next to each other on the bleachers.
4. The <u>cheerleaders</u> (or) the basketball <u>players</u> will act as ushers.
5. <u>Singing</u> (and) <u>dancing</u> will be the main events.
6. The <u>band</u> (and) the <u>bandleader</u> have practiced.
7. A <u>singer</u> (or) a <u>dancer</u> will be the featured attraction.
8. <u>Talk</u> (and) <u>laughter</u> will fill the gym.
9. The lead <u>singer</u> (and) the <u>chorus</u> sing soulfully.
10. The <u>music</u> (and) <u>dance</u> mesmerize the audience.

B. Complete each sentence with a coordinating conjunction to connect the subjects. **[Possible answers are given.]**

1. Elizabeth ___[and]___ Tina study together.
2. He ___[and, or]___ I will borrow the class notes.
3. The teacher ___[and, or]___ the aide will administer the test.
4. Not you ___[but]___ I am unprepared for this test.
5. The test ___[and]___ an answer grid were placed on my desk.

C. Complete each sentence with a compound subject. **[Possible answers are given.]**

1. ___[Adults]___ and ___[children]___ like picnics.
2. ___[Blankets]___ and ___[baskets]___ were placed on the ground.
3. Not ___[Terrence]___ but ___[Jonas]___ brought the grill.
4. I'd like ___[lemonade]___ or ___[water]___ to drink but not both.
5. ___[Singing]___ but not ___[dancing]___ goes on all afternoon.

Name _____

94. Conjunctions with Predicates

> Two or more predicates joined by a coordinating conjunction form a **compound predicate**.
>
> The picnickers <u>talked</u> <u>and</u> <u>ate</u> all afternoon.

A. Circle the conjunction in each sentence. Underline the verbs it connects.

1. I <u>awake</u> (and) <u>slide</u> out of bed.

2. I <u>wash</u> (and) <u>dry</u> my face.

3. For breakfast I <u>toast</u> some bread (or) <u>fix</u> cereal with fruit.

4. I <u>put</u> on my hat (and) <u>pull</u> on my gloves.

5. I <u>take</u> my backpack (but) often <u>carry</u> my lunch.

6. I <u>wave</u> (and) <u>yell</u> to get the bus driver's attention.

7. My friends <u>talk</u> (or) <u>sing</u> on the bus.

8. We are <u>tested</u> (and) <u>quizzed</u> on many subjects.

9. I usually <u>walk</u> (but) sometimes <u>run</u> to the bus stop.

10. The teacher <u>listens</u> (and) <u>comments</u> thoughtfully each time I talk.

B. Complete each sentence. Use a conjunction to connect the verbs.

1. The baby cried ___**[and]**___ laughed at different times today.

2. The mother hugged ___**[and]**___ kissed the baby.

3. The father did not feed ___**[but]**___ washed the baby.

4. The baby cannot walk ___**[and, or]**___ talk yet.

5. The baby's cereal heats ___**[and]**___ bubbles quickly.

C. Complete each sentence with a compound predicate. [Possible answers are given.]

1. The old car ___**[rumbles]**___ and ___**[creaks]**___.

2. We ___**[washed]**___ and ___**[waxed]**___ it.

3. Afterward it ___**[glistened]**___ and ___**[shone]**___ in the sun.

4. We ___**[called]**___ and ___**[waved]**___ to our friends as we drove it through town.

5. It ___**[spat]**___ and ___**[sputtered]**___ when we changed gears.

Name _____

95. Conjunctions with Direct Objects

> A verb that has two or more direct objects has a **compound direct object.** The parts of a compound direct object are connected by a coordinating conjunction.
>
> **The carpenter carried a hammer and a saw.**

A. Circle the conjunction in each sentence. Underline the direct objects it connects.

1. Airplanes transport mail (and) passengers.

2. Many passengers like takeoff (but) not landing.

3. Flight attendants offer food (and) drinks to passengers.

4. Meals usually include beef (or) chicken.

5. Passengers often have cell phones (and) laptop computers.

6. Flight attendants explain safety precautions (and) flight rules.

7. They also mention seat belts (and) floatation devices.

8. Often a flight attendant must practice patience (and) kindness with a troublesome passenger.

9. The pilot announces the plane's current location (and) its estimated time of arrival.

10. Flight attendants provide not entertainment (but) safety.

B. Complete each sentence. Use a conjunction to connect the direct objects. **[Possible answers are given.]**

1. The model was wearing a blue coat ___[and]___ a hat.

2. She applied powder ___[and]___ blush to her face.

3. Her agent didn't like her makeup ___[and, or]___ her clothes.

4. The photographer scrutinized the shadows ___[and]___ light on the model's face.

5. The model offered not frowns ___[but]___ smiles to the camera.

C. Complete each sentence with a compound direct object. **[Possible answers are given.]**

1. For a first course we're offered ___[salad]___ but not ___[soup]___.

2. The waiter will serve ___[pie]___ and ___[cake]___ for dessert.

3. We left our ___[coats]___ and ___[hats]___ at the coat check.

4. We could take a ___[bus]___ or a ___[taxi]___ home.

5. We could watch ___[TV]___ or a ___[video]___ once we got home.

96. Conjunctions with Subject Complements

> A sentence that has two or more subject complements has a **compound subject complement.** The parts of a compound subject complement are connected by a coordinating conjunction.
>
> **Our study of the original colonies was <u>interesting</u> and <u>enlightening</u>.**

A. Circle the coordinating conjunction in each sentence. Underline the subject complements it connects.

1. Many of the original colonists were <u>farmers</u> (or) <u>trappers</u>.

2. The soil in New England was <u>thin</u> (and) <u>rocky</u>.

3. Winters were very <u>cold</u> (and) <u>snowy</u>.

4. Some of New England's primary goods were <u>lumber</u> (and) <u>fish</u>.

5. Its manufactured products were <u>ships</u> (and) <u>clothing</u>.

6. The main foods raised in the Middle Colonies were <u>vegetables</u> (and) <u>grain</u>.

7. The soil in these colonies was <u>rich</u> (and) <u>fertile</u>.

8. Summer in the Southern Colonies was <u>hot</u> (and) <u>humid</u>.

9. The main crops grown in the Southern Colonies were <u>rice</u> (and) <u>tobacco</u>.

10. Some of the native people were the <u>Algonquin</u> (and) the <u>Wampanoag</u>.

B. Complete each sentence with a conjunction to connect the subject complements. **[Possible answers are given.]**

1. The founders of most of the colonies were English __[or]__ Dutch.

2. The settlers were brave __[and]__ energetic.

3. Their main needs were food __[and]__ tools.

4. The things they desired were land __[and]__ freedom.

5. The native people they met could be friends __[or]__ enemies.

C. Complete each sentence with a compound subject complement. **[Answers will vary.]**

1. My favorite subjects are _____ and _____.

2. I like them because they are _____ and _____.

3. My best friends are _____ and _____.

4. My friends like me because I am _____ and _____.

5. My favorite hobbies are _____ and _____.

Prepositions, Conjunctions, Interjections

97. Conjunctions with Sentences

> Sentences can be connected by a conjunction. Two complete sentences joined by a coordinating conjunction form a **compound sentence**.
>
> **I kept the sturdy raincoat, <u>but</u> I returned the flimsy jacket.**

A. Read the two sentences in each example. Add a conjunction to connect the two sentences. Use *and, but,* or *or.* In some cases, more than one conjunction may be correct.

1. Diamonds are precious gems, __[but]__ they are also used for industry.

2. You can wear diamonds on your fingers, __[and]__ you can use diamonds to cut glass.

3. The diamond was insured, __[but]__ she was still afraid to wear it.

4. You must clean and polish your diamond ring, __[or]__ it will look dull.

5. A cubic zirconia may look like a diamond, __[but]__ it doesn't cost as much.

6. The diamond is not my birthstone, __[but]__ I want one anyway.

7. Her diamond was square, __[and]__ it had sapphires on its sides.

8. She might give the diamond ring to her daughter, __[or]__ she might donate it to charity.

9. The diamond shimmered, __[and]__ its gold setting shone.

10. She wore no diamonds or gold, __[but]__ she looked like a princess anyway.

B. Circle the conjunction in each sentence. Underline the words the conjunction connects. Write on the line whether the conjunction connects subjects, verbs, direct objects, subject complements, or sentences.

__[direct objects]__ 1. Our class art project on color required paint (and) water.

__[direct objects]__ 2. First we filled jars (and) glasses with water.

__[direct objects]__ 3. Next we gathered paints (and) brushes together.

__[subjects]__ 4. Paper (and) charts were hung around the room.

__[subjects]__ 5. Then the boys (and) the girls had a contest.

__[direct objects]__ 6. Trudy mixed blue (and) yellow to make green.

__[subject complements]__ 7. The colors Ted used were red (and) blue.

__[verbs]__ 8. He mixed (and) blended the colors to get violet.

__[direct objects]__ 9. Tara mixed red (and) green together.

__[sentences]__ 10. It didn't look like a color, (but) it did look like mud!

Name _____

98. Subordinate Conjunctions

> A clause has a subject and a predicate. An independent clause expresses a complete thought and can stand alone as a sentence. A dependent clause does not express a complete thought and cannot stand alone as a sentence. A **subordinate conjunction** introduces a dependent clause and connects it to the independent clause. Many subordinate conjunctions tell *when*. They include *after, as, as soon as, before, once, since, when, whenever, while,* and *until.*
>
> <u>After</u> the Civil War ended, African Americans looked for business opportunities.
> Many women worked as maids <u>until</u> they could find better jobs.

Circle the subordinate conjunction in each sentence.

1. Sarah Breedlove was orphaned (when) she was seven years old.

2. She married and had a daughter (while) she was just a teenager.

3. (After) her husband died, Sarah moved to St. Louis.

4. She worked as a washerwoman (until) a scalp ailment made her hair fall out.

5. (After) trying several hair treatments, she realized that there were few hair products especially for African American women.

6. (When) she tried products made by another black woman, her scalp condition improved.

7. (As soon as) she could, she started selling hair products to black women.

8. (After) Sarah moved to Denver in 1905, she married C. J. Walker.

9. (Once) they became business partners, she changed her name to Madame C. J. Walker.

10. (After) creating her own line of products, Walker began selling them door-to-door.

11. (As) the business grew, Madame Walker hired other women to sell her products.

12. She continued to work hard (until) she had more than 3,000 employees.

13. (After) years of struggling, Madame Walker became America's first self-made female millionaire.

14. (Whenever) she found a good cause, she donated money to it.

15. (Since) her death in 1919, she has been regarded as a role model by many women.

Madame C. J. Walker worked hard to become a successful businessperson. Give an example of how you can work hard to be successful at something.

99. Interjections

An **interjection** expresses a strong feeling or emotion. Listed below are some common interjections and the emotions they could express.

JOY	Hurrah! Bravo! Great! Oh!	WONDER	Ah! Oh!
DISGUST	Oh! Ick! Yuck! Ugh!	SORROW	Oh! Ah!
CAUTION	Hush! Shh! Uh-oh!	IMPATIENCE	Goodness! Well!
PAIN	Oh! Ouch!	SURPRISE	What! Oh! Aha! Wow!

A. Underline the interjections. Write on the line what emotion each interjection expresses. [**Possible answers are given.**]

____[joy]____ 1. <u>Great!</u> You're here.

____[impatience]____ 2. <u>Well!</u> We should be in our seats by now.

____[wonder]____ 3. <u>Oh!</u> This opera house is magnificent.

____[pain]____ 4. <u>Ouch!</u> This seat isn't comfortable.

____[caution]____ 5. <u>Uh-oh!</u> The first act is about to begin.

____[sorrow]____ 6. <u>Oh!</u> The story is terribly sad.

____[wonder]____ 7. <u>Ah!</u> Her voice is really beautiful.

____[surprise]____ 8. <u>What!</u> It's almost over.

____[caution]____ 9. <u>Shh!</u> They're still singing.

____[joy]____ 10. They sang so well. <u>Bravo!</u>

B. Write appropriate interjections on the lines. [**Possible answers are given.**]

____[Uh-oh!]____ 1. Move out of the way of the bus.

____[Ick!]____ 2. It splashed me with that mucky water.

____[Oh!]____ 3. My coat is ruined.

____[What!]____ 4. You have a clean one I can borrow?

____[Hurrah!]____ 5. Now we can still go out.

____[Oh!]____ 6. I don't think I can go.

____[Uh-oh!]____ 7. Is something the matter?

____[Oh!]____ 8. I have a terrible headache.

____[Aha!]____ 9. I thought you weren't acting like your usual cheerful self.

____[Ah!]____ 10. We'll miss you if you go home.

Prepositions, Conjunctions, Interjections

Name _____

100. Reviewing Prepositions, Conjunctions, and Interjections

A. Circle the preposition in each sentence.
Underline the prepositional phrase.

1. The lawyer walked (toward) the courthouse.
2. The papers (in) his briefcase were exhibits.
3. He got home quite late every night (during) the trial.
4. The judge sat (inside) his chambers.
5. They put the defendant (on) the stand.

B. Circle the correct preposition in parentheses.

6. The shirts were distributed (between (among)) the members of the team.
7. Just ((between) among) you and me, I don't like them.
8. Their color is somewhere ((between) among) green and yellow.
9. We bought them ((from) off) a dealer for a reduced price.
10. I'll never take it (from (off)) if we win a game.

C. Write on the lines below whether each *italicized* phrase is used as an adjective or an adverb.

The tree *on the hill* was struck *by lightning*. The mishap occurred
           11.   **12.**

during a violent storm. It was a hot day *in August*. The dark clouds rolled
     13.   **14.**

across the sky. Raindrops *of enormous size* pelted the countryside. Thunder
     15.   **16.**

echoed *with loud booms*, and lightning darted *across the heavens*. It lasted
       17.   **18.**

for a short time only. Then the dark clouds were replaced *by blue sky*.
       19.   **20.**

11. _____[adjective]_____   16. _____[adjective]_____
12. _____[adverb]_____   17. _____[adverb]_____
13. _____[adverb]_____   18. _____[adverb]_____
14. _____[adjective]_____   19. _____[adverb]_____
15. _____[adverb]_____   20. _____[adverb]_____

 CONTINUED

Name _____

D. Write on the line whether the *italicized* conjunction connects
subjects, verbs, direct objects, subject complements, or sentences.

_____[subjects]_____ 21. Mike Fink *and* Paul Bunyan are folk heroes.

_____[verbs]_____ 22. People tell *and* retell stories about them.

_____[direct objects]_____ 23. They performed amazing feats *and* heroic deeds.

_____[sentences]_____ 24. Mike had a great appetite, *but* Paul could eat more.

_____[verbs]_____ 25. For breakfast Paul ate 100 pancakes *and* drank 14 gallons of milk.

_____[direct objects]_____ 26. Paul farmed the Rocky Mountain Valley *and* the Colorado River Valley.

_____[direct objects]_____ 27. He used Babe the Blue Ox *and* a huge plow.

_____[subjects]_____ 28. Mike *or* Paul would have helped anyone.

_____[subject complements]_____ 29. They were strong *but* kind.

_____[sentences]_____ 30. Both have died, *but* their memories live on.

E. Write appropriate interjections on the lines. **[Answers will vary.]**

_____[Shh!]_____ 31. Mike Fink is aiming for the mosquito on the fence.

_____[What!]_____ 32. Did Mike jump across the Ohio River?

_____[Wow!]_____ 33. Those two were amazing.

_____[Hush!]_____ 34. She's telling the story of another folk hero.

_____[Great!]_____ 35. I love these stories.

Try It Yourself.
Write three sentences about your favorite folktale character. Use prepositional
phrases, conjunctions, and at least one interjection in your sentences.

_____

_____

_____

Check Your Own Work
Choose a selection from your writing portfolio, your journal, a work
in progress, an assignment from another class, or a letter. Revise it,
applying the skills you have reviewed. This checklist will help you.

✔ Have you used appropriate prepositions?

✔ Have you used *between*, *among*, *from*, and *off* correctly?

✔ Have you used interjections that express the correct emotions?

Prepositions, Conjunctions, Interjections

Name _____

101. Complete Sentences

A **sentence** is a group of words that expresses a complete thought.
Every sentence has a subject and a predicate.

SUBJECT   PREDICATE

That busy lawyer   devotes some of her time to charity work.

**A. Read each example. Write S on the line if the words form a sentence.
Write NS on the line if the words do not form a sentence.**

__[NS]__ 1. Many years ago.

__[S]__ 2. Most pioneers traveled in covered wagons.

__[NS]__ 3. Sometimes large families and even a dog.

__[NS]__ 4. Early in the morning.

__[S]__ 5. They made bread in cast iron pans.

__[NS]__ 6. Often slept under their wagons.

__[S]__ 7. Some of the wagons were pulled by oxen.

__[NS]__ 8. Met Indians on the plains.

__[NS]__ 9. Became sick on their journey.

__[NS]__ 10. No doctor to help them.

__[NS]__ 11. The dangerous snow-covered mountains.

__[S]__ 12. The deserts were very hard on the animals.

__[S]__ 13. Occasionally the pioneers became lost.

__[S]__ 14. Many of the pioneers were immigrants.

__[NS]__ 15. Founded new towns out west.

**B. Write a complete sentence, using each group of words.
Be sure to start each sentence with a capital letter and
end it with the correct punctuation mark. [Sentences will vary.]**

when it rains   1. _____

alone at night   2. _____

in the attic   3. _____

is scary   4. _____

in the mirror   5. _____

Name _____

102. Four Kinds of Sentences

There are four kinds of sentences:
declarative, interrogative, imperative, and exclamatory.

A **declarative sentence** makes a statement. It ends with a period.

The weather is beautiful today.

An **interrogative sentence** asks a question. It ends with a question mark.

Will I need my umbrella?

An **imperative sentence** gives a command or makes a request.
It ends with a period. The subject is generally understood to be *you.*

Wear this waterproof jacket.

An **exclamatory sentence** expresses strong emotion.
It ends with an exclamation point.

I told you not to go out in the rain!

Add the end punctuation to each sentence. Decide if the sentence
is declarative, interrogative, imperative, or exclamatory.
Write your answer on the line. [**Some answers may vary.**]

[interrogative]   1. Have you ever read Greek mythology?

[imperative]   2. Name some of the ancient gods and goddesses.

[exclamatory]   3. How fascinating the stories are!

[declarative]   4. My favorite myth is about Medusa.

[interrogative]   5. Do you know the god of war?

[declarative]   6. Pegasus is a horse with wings.

[imperative]   7. Name a mythological creature.

[exclamatory]   8. How mighty Zeus was!

[interrogative]   9. Is Venus the goddess of love?

[exclamatory]   10. What a fearsome creature is the Minotaur!

[interrogative]   11. Who was the boy who tried to fly?

[declarative]   12. Hercules was a Greek hero known for his great strength.

[imperative]   13. List Hercules' 12 labors.

[exclamatory]   14. How angry Hera gets!

[interrogative]   15. Did Argus, the hundred-eyed monster, see you?

Sentences

103. Simple Subjects and Simple Predicates

The **subject** names the person, place, or thing that the sentence is about.
The **simple subject** is a pronoun or a noun without any of its modifiers.

> The kind young <u>man</u> helped the elderly woman across the street.

The **predicate** tells what the subject is or does. The **simple predicate** is a verb or a verb phrase without any of its modifiers, objects, or complements.

> The kind young man <u>helped</u> the elderly woman across the street.

Read each sentence. Underline the simple subject and circle the simple predicate.

1. <u>Norman Rockwell</u> (is) one of the most well-known American artists.

2. <u>He</u> (lived) first in New York and then in Vermont.

3. <u>He</u> (enrolled) in art school at the age of 14.

4. The <u>Boy Scouts of America</u> (hired) him in his late teens as the art director of its publication *Boys' Life*.

5. <u>He</u> (painted) 321 magazine covers for *The Saturday Evening Post*.

6. <u>Rockwell</u> (supported) civil rights and the exploration of space.

7. <u>He</u> also (cared) about poverty in America.

8. <u>Some</u> of his paintings (illustrate) these things.

9. <u>Most</u> of Rockwell's works (depict) everyday America.

10. <u>Rockwell's subjects</u> (include) dogs and children, baseball and barbershops.

 Norman Rockwell painted and illustrated everyday America, but he also depicted things that interested or concerned him. He wanted other people to care about these things too. Give an example of how you can share one of your interests or concerns.

Sentences

Name _____

104. Complete Subjects

> The subject with all its modifiers is called the **complete subject**.
>
> **The street artist with his guitar and harmonica entertained the tourists passing by.**

A. Read each sentence. Circle the simple subject and underline the complete subject.

1. The Jamestown (colonists) arrived in America in 1607.

2. The 104 male (settlers) in Jamestown had many problems.

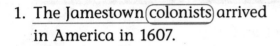

3. The (water) near the town was bad for drinking.

4. Many dangerous (insects) lived around the swampy colony.

5. Insect (bites) caused disease among the settlers.

6. The (men) in the colony didn't know how to hunt or fish.

7. The (people) of Jamestown asked John Smith to be their leader.

8. The resourceful (Smith) helped the people work together to survive.

9. The grateful (colonists) began to store food for the winter.

10. Some helpful (American Indians) taught the colonists to grow corn.

B. Complete each sentence with a descriptive adjective or an adjective phrase. Put parentheses around the complete subjects. **[Possible answers are given.]**

1. (The ice _____ [on the pond] _____) has thawed.

2. (The ice skates _____ [in the closet] _____) can't be used.

3. (The _____ [deep] _____ snow) has almost disappeared.

4. (The trees _____ [in the neighborhood] _____) will soon have tiny buds.

5. (The birds _____ [down south] _____) will soon fly north.

Name _____

105. Complete Predicates

> The predicate with all its modifiers, objects, and complements is called the **complete predicate**.
>
> **The hungry child ate pizza, pasta, and salad for dinner.**

A. Read each sentence. Circle the simple predicate and underline the complete predicate.

1. Most of the settlers in the New England colonies (arrived) there from England.

2. They (lived) in villages like their old ones in England.

3. Many villages (had) a meeting house in the center.

4. The settlers (used) the meeting house as a church.

5. They (talked) about village problems there.

6. The Middle Colonies (had) good land for farming.

7. The people in these colonies (came) from many different lands.

8. The colonists (did) not all (practice) the same religious faith.

9. Colonists in New York (spoke) 18 different languages.

10. Colonists in the Middle Colonies (sold) wheat to people in other colonies.

B. Complete the sentences with modifiers, objects, or complements. Put parentheses around the complete predicates. **[Possible answers given.]**

1. Thomas (was given _____[the athletic award.])

2. Ken (ate _____[pancakes and sausage for breakfast.])

3. Catherine (wrote _____[the essay.])

4. Lightning (streaked _____[across the sky.])

5. The tourists (crowded _____[into the bus.])

6. Mike (told _____[me the secret.])

7. Weeds (grew _____[in the flower garden.])

8. The car (stopped _____[at the corner.])

9. The terrier (bounded _____[across the field.])

10. The pilot (climbed _____[into the plane.])

Sentences

111

106. Direct Objects and Indirect Objects

> The **direct object** is a noun or a pronoun that answers the question *whom* or *what* after an action verb.
>
> **In 1985 three-year-old Lang Lang began playing the <u>piano</u>.**
>
> The **indirect object** tells *to whom, for whom, to what,* or *for what* an action is done. The indirect object comes between the action verb and the direct object.
>
> **Professor Zhu Ya-Fen gave <u>Lang Lang</u> his first piano lessons.**

A. **Underline the direct object in each sentence.**

1. At age five Lang Lang won first <u>prize</u> in the Shenyang Piano Competition.

2. Soon after that he gave his first piano <u>recital</u>.

3. He won a piano <u>competition</u> in Germany at age 11.

4. At 14 he performed a <u>piece</u> with the China National Symphony.

5. The next year he began his <u>studies</u> in Philadelphia.

B. **Circle the indirect object in each sentence. The direct object is underlined.**

1. Lang Lang's father taught (him) traditional Chinese <u>music</u>.

2. Lang Lang gave his (father) the <u>opportunity</u> to play Chinese music in America.

3. The United Nations offered (Lang Lang) the <u>position</u> of Goodwill Ambassador.

4. Lang Lang gives (children) of the world his <u>support</u>.

5. On *Sesame Street* Lang Lang showed (Elmo) the <u>benefits</u> of exercising to music.

C. **Underline the direct object in each sentence. Circle the indirect object.**

1. Mrs. Carter teaches (students) <u>music</u> at Hawthorn School.

2. She assigned (Carla) a <u>piece</u> by Mozart.

3. Carla gave (Mrs. Carter) her full <u>attention</u>.

4. Harold showed (Paul) his new <u>guitar</u>.

5. Paul promised (Harold) some <u>help</u> after rehearsal.

6. Maria lent (Inez) a <u>copy</u> of the song.

7. Mrs. Carter bought the (class) <u>tickets</u> to a concert.

8. She offered (them) the <u>opportunity</u> to hear professional musicians.

9. The students wrote (Mrs. Carter) a <u>letter</u> of thanks.

10. They paid (her) many <u>compliments</u>.

Sentences

107. Subject Complements

> A **subject complement** completes the meaning of a linking verb. It is part of the predicate. If the subject complement is a noun, it renames the subject. If the subject complement is an adjective, it describes the subject.
>
> **Anne Sullivan was an orphan.**
> **She was almost blind.**

A. Circle the subject complement in each sentence. Write **N** if it is a noun or **A** if it is an adjective.

_[N]_ 1. Anne Sullivan was the best (student) in her class at the Perkins Institute for the Blind.

_[N]_ 2. Helen Keller was a deaf and blind (girl.)

_[A]_ 3. She was (seven).

_[N]_ 4. Anne became Helen's (teacher.)

_[A]_ 5. Helen was very (undisciplined.)

_[A]_ 6. She was (unable) to communicate with her parents.

_[N]_ 7. Anne was a great (help) to Helen.

_[A]_ 8. She was (patient) with Helen.

_[N]_ 9. Helen became a good (student) who could read Braille.

_[A]_ 10. People were (amazed) at Anne's work.

_[A]_ 11. Anne was (proud) when Helen graduated from college.

_[N]_ 12. Her graduation was a great (accomplishment.)

_[A]_ 13. Anne and Helen were (happy) to raise money for the American Foundation for the Blind.

_[N]_ 14. They were a great (success) at giving lectures.

_[N]_ 15. The two women were lifelong (friends.)

B. Complete each sentence with a noun or an adjective used as a subject complement. [Answers will vary.]

1. My favorite food is _____.

2. I like that food because it is _____.

3. My least favorite food is _____.

4. I don't like that food because it is _____.

5. The best meal I ever ate was _____.

Sentences

108. Sentence Order

> A sentence is in **natural order** when the verb follows the subject.
>
> **The little house stood on the prairie.**
>
> A sentence is in **inverted order** when the verb or a helping verb comes before the subject.
>
> **On the prairie stood the little house.**

Underline the simple subject and circle the simple predicate. Write N if the sentence is in natural order and I if the sentence is in inverted order.

___[I]___ 1. Many centuries ago (lived) the Anasazi.

___[N]___ 2. *Anasazi* (is) a Navajo word meaning "ancient ones."

___[N]___ 3. Some of their ruins (are) in Colorado's Mesa Verde National Park.

___[N]___ 4. In the high cliffs of the Mesa Verde area they (built) cliff dwellings.

___[I]___ 5. Four stories high (stood) some of these dwellings.

___[N]___ 6. The Anasazi (used) ladders to enter their cliff homes.

___[I]___ 7. In the winter, bitterly cold (were) these homes.

___[N]___ 8. The Anasazi (were called) Basketmakers.

___[N]___ 9. They (excelled) at basketry.

___[I]___ 10. Waterproof (were) some of their baskets.

___[N]___ 11. The archaeologists (dug) under the kiva, a community's underground room.

___[I]___ 12. Through the kiva (whipped) the wind.

___[I]___ 13. Below the cliff dwellings (lies) a trash area.

___[N]___ 14. Piñon pines and juniper trees (grew) in the area.

___[N]___ 15. The Anasazi farms (lay) on top of the mesa.

Name _____

109. Compound Subjects

> If a sentence has two or more simple subjects joined by a coordinating conjunction, it is said to have a **compound subject**.
>
> **The student and the teacher discussed the assignment.**

A. Read each sentence. Underline the compound subject.
Circle the conjunction.

1. Grapes (and) peaches grow on that farm.
2. Fruits (and) vegetables are good sources of vitamins.
3. Not Brendan (but) Juan fed apples to the horses.
4. California (and) Florida have many orange groves.
5. Strawberries (and) rhubarb were the ingredients.
6. Carrots (and) sweet potatoes are orange.
7. My rabbits (and) my guinea pigs eat lettuce.
8. Insects (or) droughts can ruin vegetable crops.
9. Corn (and) pumpkins are sold at the roadside market.
10. Nicole (and) her family picked blueberries in Michigan.
11. Joan (but) not Phoebe brought a piece of fruit for lunch.
12. Cows (and) horses are kept in separate barns.
13. Ducks (and) geese swim in the pond near the farm.
14. Broccoli (or) carrots are good additions on a salad.
15. Corn (and) soybeans are the chief crops of Nebraska and Illinois.

B. Complete each sentence with a compound subject. [Possible answers are given.]

1. _____[Nick]_____ and _____[Alex]_____ have gone to the airport.
2. _____[Grandma]_____ and _____[Grandpa]_____ are coming to visit.
3. The _____[suitcases]_____ and the _____[wheelchair]_____ just fit in the trunk.
4. _____[They]_____ and _____[our parents]_____ will have lots to talk about.
5. _____[Dad]_____ or _____[I]_____ will take Grandpa for a walk.

Sentences

115

110. Compound Predicates

> If a sentence has two or more verbs joined by a conjunction, it is said to have a **compound predicate**.
>
> **A thief <u>stole</u> and <u>sold</u> the famous painting.**

A. Underline the compound simple predicate in each sentence. Circle the conjunction.

1. The patients <u>sat</u> (and) <u>waited</u> for the doctor.

2. Their friends and spouses <u>cheered</u> (and) <u>comforted</u> them.

3. The busy orderlies <u>came</u> (and) <u>went</u> through the emergency room doors.

4. Those doors <u>opened</u> (and) <u>closed</u> frequently.

5. The victim <u>was calmed</u> (and) then <u>was examined</u> by the doctors.

6. He <u>yelled</u> (and) <u>cried</u> in pain when they touched him.

7. The pregnant woman <u>perspired</u> (and) <u>breathed</u> hard during delivery.

8. The premature baby <u>did not kick</u> (or) <u>scream</u> as other babies do.

9. The mother <u>nurses</u> (or) <u>feeds</u> the baby with a bottle.

10. The father <u>talks</u> (and) <u>sings</u> to the baby.

B. Read the sentences. Combine each pair of sentences into one sentence with a compound predicate. **[Possible answers are given.]**

1. The teacher stacked the tests on her desk. She wrote the directions on the board.
   [The teacher stacked the tests on her desk and wrote the directions on the board.]

2. The student cleared his desk. The student sharpened his pencil.
   [The student cleared his desk and sharpened his pencil.]

3. After the test put your pencils down. After the test turn your papers over.
   [After the test put your pencils down and turn your papers over.]

4. Now we'll review our tests. Now we'll correct our mistakes.
   [Now we'll review our tests and correct our mistakes.]

5. The student reached for his test. The student smiled when he saw it.
   [The student reached for his test and smiled when he saw it.]

111. Compound Direct Objects

> If a verb has two or more direct objects, it is said to have
> a **compound direct object**.
>
> **In gym class we played** <u>basketball</u> **and floor** <u>hockey</u>**.**

A. Underline the compound direct object in each sentence.
Circle the conjunction.

1. We will visit the <u>Sears Tower</u> (or) the <u>John Hancock Building</u>
   in Chicago.

2. Visitors to New York can see the <u>Statue of Liberty</u>
   (but) not the <u>Eiffel Tower</u>.

3. In London buy a <u>postcard</u> (or) a <u>model</u> of Big Ben's clock
   tower, one of London's famous landmarks.

4. Venice's St. Mark's Square boasts many <u>tourists</u> (and) <u>pigeons</u>.

5. Can you envision Rome's <u>Colosseum</u> (and) Athens's <u>Parthenon</u>?

6. Photograph the <u>Sphinx</u> (and) the <u>Great Pyramid</u> when you tour Egypt.

7. Research <u>Falling Water</u> (or) <u>Taliesin</u> to find out about
   Frank Lloyd Wright's architecture.

8. Read the <u>rules</u> (and) <u>regulations</u> carefully before entering
   the Taj Mahal, a beautiful building in Agra, India.

9. The Eiffel Tower in Paris attracts many <u>tourists</u> (but) few <u>locals</u>.

10. See every <u>nook</u> (and) <u>cranny</u> of Sagrada Familia (Holy Family),
    a famous church in Barcelona, Spain.

B. Complete each sentence with a compound object. **[Possible answers are given.]**

1. Do you have a _____[pencil]_____ or a _____[pen]_____?

2. I am writing a short _____[story]_____ or a _____[poem]_____.

3. A writer needs _____[paper]_____ to write on or a _____[keyboard]_____
   to type on.

4. That topic makes _____[adults]_____ and _____[children]_____ alike
   think seriously.

5. Ask a _____[magazine]_____ or _____[newspaper]_____ to publish your work.

112. Compound Subject Complements

A sentence with more than one subject complement has a **compound subject complement**. Noun subject complements rename the subject of the sentence. Adjective subject complements describe the subject.

Leonardo da Vinci was an artist and an inventor.
His paintings are few but famous.

A. Underline the compound subject complement in each sentence. Write **N** if the words are nouns or **A** if the words are adjectives.

___[A]___ 1. As a boy Leonardo was handsome and charming.

___[N]___ 2. He was a good singer and musician.

___[N]___ 3. He was also a vegetarian and an animal lover.

___[N]___ 4. At age 15 he became the helper and student of a painter.

___[A]___ 5. Leonardo was creative and skillful.

___[N]___ 6. Two of his famous paintings are *The Last Supper* and the *Mona Lisa*.

___[N]___ 7. The models were people from Milan and a lady from Florence.

___[A]___ 8. The smile on the *Mona Lisa* is small and mysterious.

___[N]___ 9. Leonardo was an engineer and an architect.

___[N]___ 10. His employers were governments and royalty.

___[A]___ 11. His inventions were clever and astonishing.

___[N]___ 12. Some of his projects were bridges and a mechanical lion.

___[N]___ 13. Other ideas were a flying machine and a submarine.

___[N]___ 14. In 1516 he became a painter and an architect for the King of France.

___[A]___ 15. Leonardo's life was long and exciting.

B. Complete each sentence with a compound subject complement. Add articles if needed. **[Answers will vary.]**

1. My favorite movies are _____ and _____.

2. My favorite kinds of TV shows are _____ and _____.

3. I would like to be _____ or _____.

4. When I work, I am _____ and _____.

5. My friends think I am _____ and _____.

Name _____

113. Compound Sentences

> A **compound sentence** contains two or more independent clauses. An independent clause has a subject and a predicate and can stand alone as a sentence. A compound sentence is formed by connecting two independent clauses with a comma and the coordinating conjunction *and, but,* or *or.* A semicolon (;) may be used instead of the comma and the conjunction.
>
> **Owls have large heads, and their eyes face forward.**
> **Owls cannot move their eyes within their eye sockets; they must move their entire heads to look around.**

A. For each of these compound sentences, draw one line under the complete subject in each independent clause and two lines under the complete predicate.

1. An owl's thick feathers absorb sound, and an owl's flight is almost silent.

2. Some owls have feathered ear tufts, but these tufts are not really ears.

3. Owls are carnivores, and most owls hunt at night.

4. An owl's keen sense of sight helps the owl navigate in the dark, and a sharp sense of hearing helps it find food.

5. Owls are at the top of a food chain; adult owls have few predators.

B. Combine each pair of sentences to make a compound sentence. Use a comma and a coordinating conjunction to combine the sentences. [Conjunctions may vary.]

1. Burrowing owls live in grasslands. These owls are unusual in many ways.
   [Burrowing owls live in grasslands, and these owls are unusual in many ways.]

2. The owls are the size of robins. They are often active in broad daylight.
   [The owls are the size of robins, and they are often active in broad daylight.]

3. An adult burrowing owl is about nine inches tall. It has a short tail and long legs.
   [An adult burrowing owl is about nine inches tall, and it has a short tail and long legs.]

4. It has a rounded head. Unlike many other owls, it does not have ear tufts.
   [It has a rounded head, but unlike many other owls, it does not have ear tufts.]

5. The burrowing owl's diet includes rodents, small birds, and eggs. It will also eat reptiles and insects.
   [The burrowing owl's diet includes rodents, small birds, and eggs, but it will also eat reptiles and insects.]

Sentences

119

114. Complex Sentences

A **complex sentence** contains one independent clause and one dependent clause. An independent clause has a subject and a predicate and can stand alone as a sentence. A dependent clause has a subject and a predicate but cannot stand alone as a sentence. A subordinate conjunction introduces a dependent clause and connects it to the independent clause. Many dependent clauses tell *when.* They are introduced by subordinate conjunctions such as *after, as, as soon as, before, once, since, when, whenever, while,* and *until.*

> **Few white people lived in the Dakota Territory when Crazy Horse was born. As Crazy Horse grew up, he earned a reputation for skill and daring.**

Underline the independent clause in each complex sentence once. Underline the dependent clause twice. Circle the subordinate conjunction.

1. (Before) the Civil War was fought, the Sioux controlled a vast area of land.

2. Miners and prospectors moved to South Dakota's Black Hills (after) gold was discovered there.

3. (As) more settlers arrived, the U.S. War Department ordered the nomadic Sioux and Cheyenne to reservations.

4. (When) they heard the order, Crazy Horse and Sitting Bull refused to obey.

5. (After) a party of Sioux and Cheyenne defeated a band of U.S. soldiers, Lieutenant Colonel George A. Custer led an attack against the tribes.

6. (When) the battle was over, Custer and half of his men were dead.

7. The Army pursued the Indians (until) they were forced to surrender and move to a reservation.

8. (When) Crazy Horse's wife got sick, he took her to visit her parents at another reservation.

9. (As soon as) the soldiers heard that Crazy Horse had left, they followed him and arrested him.

10. Crazy Horse died (after) one of the soldiers stabbed him with a bayonet.

Crazy Horse stood up for what he believed in. Give an example of how you can stand up for what you believe.

Name _____

115. Reviewing Sentences

A. Read each sentence. Write **CS** if the *italicized* words are
a complete subject or **CP** if they are a complete predicate.
Write your answers on the lines.

___[CS]___ 1. *A ferocious mile-wide tornado* descended upon the town.

___[CP]___ 2. Debris *swirled around its funnel cloud.*

___[CP]___ 3. Its loud roar *echoed in the night.*

___[CP]___ 4. Trees and buildings *were leveled by its winds.*

___[CS]___ 5. *Its massive force* tore homes into pieces.

B. Read each sentence. Write **S** on the line if
the words form a sentence. Write **NS** on the line
if the words do not form a sentence.

___[NS]___ 6. Skipping through the woods
on a spring morning.

___[S]___ 7. The wolf peered from behind a tree.

___[S]___ 8. Each flower caught Little Red Riding
Hood's attention.

___[NS]___ 9. A large bouquet for Grandmother.

___[S]___ 10. To Grandmother's house she went.

C. Write on the line **declarative, interrogative, imperative,** or **exclamatory**
to tell what kind of sentence is shown. Then underline the simple subject and
circle the simple predicate. Remember that the subject of an imperative sentence
is understood to be *you.*

_____[declarative]_____ 11. Atalanta (ran) far ahead of Hippomenes.

_____[interrogative]_____ 12. (Could) Hippomenes possibly (win)?

_____[imperative]_____ 13. (Help) me now, Venus.

_____[declarative]_____ 14. The youth (threw) a golden apple far ahead.

_____[exclamatory]_____ 15. Ah, it (caught) Atalanta's attention!

CONTINUED

_____[interrogative]_____ 16. (Would) she (pick) up the apple?

_____[exclamatory]_____ 17. Yes, Atalanta (did!)

_____[imperative]_____ 18. (Take) advantage of this, Hippomenes.

_____[declarative]_____ 19. Hippomenes and Atalanta (were) side by side.

_____[declarative]_____ 20. Hippomenes (aimed) and (threw) the remaining apples.

D. Read each sentence. Write **CS** if the *italicized* words form
a compound subject, **CP** if they form a compound predicate,
or **CO** if they form a compound object. Write your answers on the lines.

Write **N** over the sentence if it is in natural order
or **I** if it is in inverted order.

_[CS]_ 21. Inside Atalanta's mind fought good [I]
     judgment and *foolishness.*

_[CP]_ 22. She *wavered* and *picked* them up. [N]

_[CO]_ 23. Hippomenes saw *hope* and *victory* [N]
     within his grasp.

_[CP]_ 24. He *reached* and *crossed* the finish line first. [N]

_[CO]_ 25. He had won for himself a *race* and a *bride!* [N]

Try It Yourself
Write four sentences about a game or contest you have seen.
Be sure to use complete sentences and correct punctuation.

_____

_____

_____

_____

Check Your Own Work
Choose a selection from your writing portfolio, your journal,
a work in progress, an assignment from another class, or a letter.
Revise it, applying the skills you have reviewed. This checklist
will help you.

✔ Do all your sentences express a complete thought?

✔ Have you used a variety of sentences—declarative, interrogative,
imperative, and exclamatory?

Sentences

Name _____

116. End Punctuation

> A declarative sentence makes a statement. An imperative sentence gives a command. Use a **period** at the end of a declarative or an imperative sentence. An interrogative sentence asks a question. Use a **question mark** at the end of an interrogative sentence. An exclamatory sentence expresses strong emotion. Use an **exclamation point** at the end of an exclamatory sentence.
>
> **Charles Dickens wrote *A Christmas Carol*.**
> **Please read it aloud.**
> **What happens to Tiny Tim?**
> **What a great story!**

Add the correct end punctuation to each sentence. [Answers may vary.]

1. Charles Dickens is a well-known English author.

2. When was he born?

3. He was born in Portsmouth on February 7, 1812.

4. What was his childhood like?

5. His family was very poor.

6. When he was 12, he had to get a job in a factory.

7. How awful that was!

8. In 1836 Dickens married Catherine Hogarth.

9. The couple had 10 children.

10. What a large family!

11. What did Dickens do besides writing?

12. He edited magazines and gave lectures.

13. He had a lot of energy.

14. He would often walk 30 miles.

15. That's amazing!

16. In 1842 Dickens visited the United States.

17. What states did he visit?

18. He traveled as far south as Virginia and as far west as Illinois.

19. He wrote *American Notes* about his journey.

20. Read one of his books for your book report.

Name _____

117. Commas in Series

> **Commas** are used to separate three or more items in a series. A comma is placed before the coordinating conjunction at the end of the series. A series may consist of all nouns, all verbs, all adverbs, all adjectives, or all phrases.
>
> **Please pick up some bread, butter, and bananas at the store.**
> **My mom, my dad, or my brother will cook dinner tonight.**

A. Add commas where needed.

1. You should never skip breakfast, lunch, or dinner.

2. Mom used her Irish linen, her German china, and her English silver.

3. Jacob put cereal, juice, yogurt, and bagels on the table.

4. Mom served cherry streusel, banana cream pie, and cheese coffeecake.

5. Quinn can prepare scrambled, poached, and hardboiled eggs.

6. In the picnic basket were sandwiches, fruit, pretzels, and lemonade.

7. Dad bought carrots, lettuce, radishes, and cucumbers for the salad.

8. The recipe said to chop, mix, season, and cook the ingredients.

9. Celery, lettuce, and peppers are my favorite vegetables.

10. Martha stretched, pulled, kneaded, and rolled out the dough.

11. Nathan, Katie, and Elizabeth will bring dessert for the picnic.

12. Is the bread on the counter, in the cupboard, or in the refrigerator?

13. My sisters, my mother, and my aunts are all excellent cooks.

14. The recipe says to stir the mixture slowly, carefully, and thoroughly.

15. The plums are sweet, juicy, and delicious.

B. Complete each sentence with a series of nouns, verbs, or adjectives. Add commas where needed. **[Answers will vary.]**

1. _____[Noun,]_____ _____[noun,]_____ and _____[noun]_____ are my favorite rides at the amusement park.

2. I saw _____[noun,]_____ _____[noun,]_____ and _____[noun]_____ at the fairgrounds.

3. Did you _____[verb,]_____ _____[verb,]_____ or _____[verb]_____ at the beach?

4. The water slide was _____[adjective,]_____ _____[adjective,]_____ and _____[adjective]_____ .

5. In the winter I _____[verb,]_____ _____[verb,]_____ and _____[verb]_____ for fun.

118. Commas with Conjunctions

> Commas are used before the conjunctions *and*, *but*, and *or* when two simple sentences are combined.
>
> **Some of the children went to art class, but others went to the gym.**

A. Read each sentence. Add commas where needed.

1. Marie likes to use paint for her art, and Erica likes to use pastels.

2. She redrew the figure, but it still wasn't right.

3. We will finish our paintings in class, or we will finish them at home.

4. The critic didn't like her drawings, but he liked her sculptures.

5. They put their paints away, and then they cleaned their brushes.

B. Read each sentence. Use a conjunction to complete each sentence. Add commas where needed.

1. Fold your paper into four equal parts _____ [, and] _____ then you can draw a favorite book character in each section.

2. I will draw Huck Finn in one of the sections _____ [, and *or*, but] _____ I don't know who will go in the other sections.

3. Huck had a friend named Jim _____ [, or] _____ was his name John?

4. Read *Huckleberry Finn* _____ [, or] _____ you will miss a good story.

5. Mark Twain wrote *Huckleberry Finn* _____ [, and *or*, but] _____ that is not all he wrote.

C. Combine each set of simple sentences with a conjunction. Add commas where needed. **[Answers may vary.]**

1. There was a long wait to ride the roller coaster. You could get on the bumper cars immediately.
   [There was a long wait to ride the roller coaster, but you could get on the bumper cars immediately.]

2. Don't eat too much food. You might feel ill on the rides.
   [Don't eat too much food, or you might feel ill on the rides.]

3. We ate lunch. Then we went on the train ride.
   [We ate lunch, and then we went on the train ride.]

4. Henry's favorite ride is the Wild Eagle. Julia enjoys the Twirly Whirly.
   [Henry's favorite ride is the Wild Eagle, and Julia enjoys the Twirly Whirly.]

5. The Wild Eagle is fun. The Twirly Whirly can be scary.
   [The Wild Eagle is fun, but the Twirly Whirly can be scary.]

119. Direct Address and Yes and No

Commas are used to separate words in direct address. When the name of a person addressed is the first word of a sentence, it is followed by a comma. If it is the last word of a sentence, a comma is placed before the name.

Tony, let's go.   **What is this thing, Sarah?**

If the name of the person is used within a sentence, one comma is placed before the name and one after the name.

I hope you know, Gina, how much I appreciate your help.

Commas are used after the words *yes* and *no* when either introduces a sentence.

Yes, you may go bike riding.   **No, it's too late to go out.**

A. **Read each sentence. Add commas where needed.**

1. Yes, seals and penguins can be found in Antarctic waters.
2. Seals, Jackie, have a layer of fat that keeps them warm in cold water.
3. Did you read the chapter on animals of the Antarctic, Kevin?
4. Boys and girls, can you name some kinds of seals?
5. No, not all seals have external ears.
6. Trina, the female seal is called a cow.
7. Can you tell me what the male seal is called, class?
8. Yes, the male seal is called a bull.
9. Usually, Eric, the cow has just one pup per breeding season.
10. Yes, the leopard seal sometimes feeds on penguins.
11. Penguins live in groups called rookeries, Paige.
12. The male penguins, David, hold the eggs on their feet.
13. No, the females do not guard the eggs.
14. Yes, penguins are heavy birds.
15. That makes them good divers and swimmers, Colette.

B. **Complete each sentence with a noun in direct address. Use correct punctuation.** **[Answers will vary.]**

1. Ernest Shackleton ___**[, Name,]**___ explored the South Pole.

2. His ship was called the *Endurance* ___**[, Name]**___ .

3. The *Endurance* ___**[, Name,]**___ got trapped in the ice.

4. Eventually ___**[, Name,]**___ the ship was crushed by the ice and sank.

5. ___**[Name,]**___ can you imagine being stranded in a lifeboat in those icy waters?

Name _____

120. Apostrophes

An **apostrophe** is used to show ownership or possession. To show that one person or thing owns something, place an apostrophe and an *s* (*'s*) after a singular noun. To show that more than one person or thing owns something, place an apostrophe after the *s* at the end of a regular plural noun. If a plural noun does not end in *-s*, place an apostrophe and an *s* (*'s*) after the noun.

The boy's bicycle is in the bike rack.
The girls' bicycles are in the bike rack.
The women's bicycles are in the bike rack.

An **apostrophe** is used in a contraction to indicate where a letter or letters have been omitted.

She's aware that I'm waiting for her.

A. Write the correct possessive form of the word to complete each sentence. Singular possessives are needed in some sentences, and plural possessives in others.

child   1. The three _____[children's]_____ trip to Everglades National Park was exciting.

park   2. Both alligators and crocodiles live in the _____[park's]_____ swamps.

alligator   3. Many _____[alligators']_____ nests lie among the roots of mangrove trees.

alligator   4. An _____[alligator's]_____ nest is a mound of vegetation.

crocodile   5. Most _____[crocodiles']_____ eggs are laid in mud or sand.

crocodile   6. They saw a _____[crocodile's]_____ eyes just above the water.

ibis   7. A white _____[ibis's]_____ bill is long and curved.

Ibis   8. _____[Ibises']_____ favorite food is crayfish.

Human   9. _____[Humans']_____ attempts to manage the water in south Florida have endangered the Everglades.

animal   10. Many _____[animals']_____ habitats are disappearing.

B. Write the contraction for each pair of words.

1. does not _____[doesn't]_____   6. I will _____[I'll]_____

2. are not _____[aren't]_____   7. we will _____[we'll]_____

3. did not _____[didn't]_____   8. you have _____[you've]_____

4. will not _____[won't]_____   9. I have _____[I've]_____

5. we have _____[we've]_____   10. you are _____[you're]_____

Name _____

121. Capital Letters

> The first word of every sentence begins with a **capital letter.** A proper noun begins with a capital letter. A proper noun names a particular person, place, or thing.
>
> the first national park in the united states was yellowstone national park.
> The first national park in the United States was Yellowstone National Park.

A. **Use the proofreading symbol (≡) under letters that should be capitalized.**

1. in 1871 ferdinand hayden led an expedition through the wyoming territory.

2. the artist thomas moran and the photographer william henry jackson accompanied him.

3. their pictures convinced congress that yellowstone should be preserved.

4. president grant signed a law in 1872 to protect yellowstone forever.

5. yellowstone is located in idaho, montana, and wyoming.

6. the most famous geyser in yellowstone is old faithful.

7. one of the smallest national parks is acadia national park in maine.

8. acadia, the first national park east of the mississippi river, was originally called lafayette national park.

9. president woodrow wilson signed legislation in 1919 that established the park.

10. acadia offers mountain hiking with views of the atlantic ocean.

11. the largest national park is wrangell–saint elias.

12. this park, located in alaska, is six times the size of yellowstone.

13. tourists to wrangell–saint elias can visit kennecott, an old copper mining town.

14. at hawaii's volcanoes national park you can see kilauea, one of the most active volcanoes in the world.

15. the kilauea cultural festival gives hawaiians an opportunity to honor their culture and traditions.

B. **Circle the groups of words that are capitalized correctly.**

1. Princeton university

2. (the Boy Scouts)

3. Mother's day

4. (Ashland Avenue)

5. (the White House)

6. (Jacqueline Bouvier Kennedy)

7. the Mississippi river

8. south Dakota

9. (the National Air and Space Museum)

10. Colorado springs, Colorado

Punctuation and Capitalization

Name _____

122. Titles

A capital letter is used for the first letter of each important word in the title of a book, movie, TV show, play, poem, song, artwork, sacred book, article, or essay. Articles, prepositions, and conjunctions are not usually capitalized. The first and last words of a title are always capitalized.

Quotation marks are used to enclose the titles of short stories, poems, and magazine articles.

| STORY | "The Scarlet Ibis" |
| POEM | "The Other Side of the Door" |

Titles of most books, magazines, plays, movies, and works of art are typed in italics. When you write the title of a book or work of art, underline the title since you cannot write in italics.

BOOK	*The Secret Garden*	The Secret Garden
MOVIE	*Star Wars*	Star Wars
PAINTING	*Starry Night*	Starry Night

A. Add the proofreading mark (=) to show which letters should be capitalized.

1. Have you read the poem "tug of war" by Kathleen Fraser?

2. Let's watch teen talent show on television tonight.

3. *the seeing summer* is a beautiful book about a blind girl.

4. Which artist painted whistling boy?

5. "valentine for earth" is a delightful poem by Frances Frost.

6. I enjoyed reading the short story "bowleg bill, cowboy of the ocean waves."

7. Does the library have the book old yeller?

8. Draw a picture after you have read the poem "subways are people."

9. The girl in the painting *girl with watering can* looks like my little sister.

10. My uncle is directing a production of the play *a raisin in the sun.*

B. Complete each sentence with appropriate information, capitalizing important words. Add quotation marks and underlining where needed. **[Answers will vary.]**

1. _____ is my favorite book.

2. Do you like the poem _____?

3. My favorite TV show is _____.

4. Our class went to the museum and saw the painting _____.

5. I just finished reading the story _____.

Punctuation and Capitalization

129

123. Other Uses of Capital Letters

A capital letter is used for the first word in a direct quotation; the directions North, South, East, and West when they refer to specific regions of a country; the pronoun *I*; titles that precede a person's name; and initials in a person's name.

Mom said, "We are going to tour the South on our vacation."
Did you know that Sir Winston Churchill's mother was an American?

A. Rewrite each phrase, using the correct capitalization.

1. famous cities of the south   [famous cities of the South]
2. president george h. w. bush   [President George H. W. Bush]
3. my cousins and i   [my cousins and I]
4. animals of the north   [animals of the North]
5. chief justice warren e. burger   [Chief Justice Warren E. Burger]
6. queen elizabeth II   [Queen Elizabeth II]
7. doctor benjamin spock   [Doctor Benjamin Spock]
8. women of the west   [women of the West]
9. j. k. rowling   [J. K. Rowling]
10. madame c. j. walker   [Madame C. J. Walker]

B. Use the proofreading symbol (≡) to show which letters should be capitalized.

1. last spring my dad said, "let's drive to the east this summer."
2. "great," my mom answered, "i have always wanted to go to washington, d.c."
3. as soon as we had decided to go, i started doing research.
4. we can hear jazz at the john f. kennedy center.
5. my brother and i want to visit the building where the supreme court meets.
6. my dad said, "i want to see the jefferson memorial."
7. he admires president jefferson for sending lewis and clark to explore the west.
8. we will be able to go to the top of the washington monument.
9. this monument honors president george washington.
10. Finally we will visit the graves of robert e. peary and matthew a. henson, two famous explorers, at arlington national cemetery.

124. Abbreviations

An **abbreviation** is a shortened form of a word. Use a period after many abbreviations. Capital letters are used for abbreviations when capital letters would be used if the words were written in full.

Reverend	Rev.	Senior	Sr.
Sunday	Sun.	January	Jan.
Street	St.	foot	ft.
before Christ	BC	after noon	p.m.

The abbreviations for terms in the metric system do not begin with capital letters and are not followed by periods. The postal abbreviations for the states have two capital letters and are not followed by periods.

meter	m	kilometer	km
Illinois	IL	Missouri	MO

A. Write the abbreviation for each of these words.

1. November   [Nov.]   6. ounce   [oz.]
2. gallon   [gal.]   7. quart   [qt.]
3. Avenue   [Ave.]   8. Junior   [Jr.]
4. Doctor   [Dr.]   9. yard   [yd.]
5. centimeter   [cm]   10. Wednesday [Wed.]

B. Rewrite each sentence. Use abbreviations whenever possible.

1. On Thursday, August 11, Doctor Irwin Stone, Junior, visited the Sears Tower.
   [On Thurs., Aug. 11, Dr. Irwin Stone, Jr., visited the Sears Tower.]

2. The building is located at 233 South Wacker Drive, Chicago, Illinois.
   [The building is located at 233 S. Wacker Dr., Chicago, IL.]

3. It is 1,454 feet, or about one-quarter mile, tall.
   [It is 1,454 ft., or about one-quarter mi., tall.]

4. Piles driven into the earth support the tower's 440 million pounds.
   [Piles driven into the earth support the tower's 440 million lb.]

5. The Sears Tower contains enough concrete to build an eight-lane highway five miles long.
   [The Sears Tower contains enough concrete to build an eight-lane highway five mi. long.]

Punctuation and Capitalization

125. Direct Quotations

A **direct quotation** restates the exact words a person has spoken. Quotation marks are used before and after a direct quotation.

> **"We have more of these in stock,"** offered the salesperson.

When a direct quotation comes at the beginning of the sentence, a comma is placed after the quotation.

> **"The story had interesting characters,"** remarked Lucy.

When a direct quotation comes at the end of the sentence, a comma is placed before the quotation.

> **The police officer warned, "Wear your seatbelts at all times."**

If the quotation ends with a question mark or exclamation point, the comma is not used.

> **"Must you wear that dirty sweatshirt?"** she asked.
> **"I won the prize!"** cried Michael.

A. Add quotation marks and other punctuation where needed.

1. "Who wants to go to the botanical gardens?" inquired William.

2. "I would like to see the spring flowers there," replied his sister Lindsay.

3. "Let's get in the car," Mom said.

4. "Buckle your seat belts," instructed Mom.

5. "This plant is quite fragile," cautioned the botanist.

6. Lindsay remarked, "It's beautiful!"

7. "Where does it grow?" asked William.

8. The botanist answered, "It grows primarily on the Pacific islands."

9. William questioned, "Like Hawaii?"

10. "Yes, it is very common there," said the botanist.

B. Complete each sentence with the exact words of the speaker. Add quotation marks and punctuation where needed. **[Answers will vary.]**

1. _____ shouted the referee.

2. Miguel announced _____.

3. Emily asked _____.

4. _____ pleaded the class.

5. _____ said the teacher.

126. More Direct Quotations

Quotation marks are used before and after every part of a divided quotation. When the exact words of the speaker are divided, more than one comma is used to separate the quotation from the rest of the sentence. Use a capital letter before the first word of a quotation, but do not use a capital letter where the quotation continues.

"King Montezuma," said the guide, "drank 50 cups of chocolate a day."

A question mark or an exclamation point that is part of the direct quotation is placed inside the quotation marks. When a question mark or an exclamation point is not part of the quotation, it is placed outside the quotation marks.

Was it Patrick Henry who said, "Give me liberty or give me death!"?
Yes, it was he who exclaimed, "Give me liberty or give me death!"

A. Add quotation marks and punctuation where needed.

1. "This is not," Paul muttered, "my favorite pastime. "

2. "Oh, really," asked Gillian, "what would you rather be doing? "

3. "I'd much rather be outside on my bike," responded Paul.

4. "Gillian," asked Paul, "wouldn't you rather be doing something else too? "

5. "Sure I would," said Gillian, "but we promised Mom we'd help her get ready for the party. "

6. "Right," agreed Paul, "we sure did. "

7. "Do you think," asked Paul, "that we've cut up enough vegetables? "

8. "Yes," said Gillian, "I think that we've prepared enough for the tray. "

9. "Now what we need to do," stated Paul, "is make the dip."

10. "No," returned Gillian, "I've already made it. "

B. Complete each sentence with the exact words of the speaker. Add quotation marks and punctuation where needed. [Answers will vary.]

1. _____ Joseph explained _____

2. _____ announced Anna _____

3. _____ said Darnell _____

4. _____ encouraged the coach _____

5. _____ the butcher replied _____

127. Addresses and Letters

In an address, capitalize the name and title of the person addressed; the name of the street and the city or town; both letters in the state's postal abbreviation; and abbreviations such as *N.* for *North,* *S.* for *South,* *E.* for *East,* and *W.* for *West.* Use a comma after the name of the city or town.

Capitalize the first word of the salutation and the first word in the complimentary close of a letter. Use a comma after the salutation of a personal letter and a colon after the salutation of a business letter. Use a comma after the closing.

2700 W. Maple Grove Ave. **Missoula, MT 59804** **May 19, 20—**	**Barton Conners** **Director of Advertising** **3660 Austrian Lane** **Green Bay, WI 54302**

A. Rewrite each phrase, adding capital letters and punctuation where needed.

1. dear uncle charley _____ [Dear Uncle Charley,]
2. all my best _____ [All my best,]
3. sincerely yours _____ [Sincerely yours,]
4. dear mrs pinkley _____ [Dear Mrs. Pinkley:]
5. january 27 2006 _____ [January 27, 2006]

B. Rewrite each address, adding capital letters and punctuation where needed.

1. dr charles j warner _____ [Dr. Charles J. Warner]
   stickly research lab _____ [Stickly Research Lab]
   3659 old mill road _____ [3659 Old Mill Road]
   canton oh 44707 _____ [Canton, OH 44707]

2. laura phelps _____ [Laura Phelps]
   gateway seed company _____ [Gateway Seed Company]
   4445 w ash street _____ [4445 W. Ash Street]
   bangor me 04401 _____ [Bangor, ME 04401]

3. doug yee, jr _____ [Doug Yee, Jr.]
   skateboards plus _____ [Skateboards Plus]
   36 e grand ave _____ [36 E. Grand Ave.]
   petaluma ca 94952 _____ [Petaluma, CA 94952]

Name _____

128. Reviewing Punctuation and Capitalization

A. **Add periods where needed.**

1. M. C. Johnson began a new business.
2. Nov. is the abbreviation for November.
3. What famous battle occurred in AD 1066?
4. Dr. Horn arrived at the hospital at 3:55 a. m.
5. Workers at the Pennsboro Electric Co. went on strike today.

B. **Write the correct abbreviation for each word.**

6.	Tuesday	[Tues.]	11.	August	[Aug.]
7.	liter	[l]	12.	Avenue	[Ave.]
8.	Captain	[Capt.]	13.	foot	[ft.]
9.	pint	[pt.]	14.	Wednesday	[Wed.]
10.	Mister	[Mr.]	15.	inch	[in.]

C. **Add commas where needed. Use the proofreading symbol (≡) under letters that should be capitalized.**

16. our first three presidents were washington, adams, and jefferson.
17. on september 17, 1796, washington delivered his famous farewell address.
18. "do not count your chickens before they are hatched," aesop advised.
19. yes, the dead sea is the saltiest.
20. do you want a sandwich, dan?

D. **Add exclamation points, question marks, and apostrophes where needed.**

21. Hurrah! The storm is over.
22. How much damage did it do?
23. I'm going to help our neighbors.
24. My father's house was not damaged.
25. What a terrible 20 minutes that was!

CONTINUED

E. **Add quotation marks where needed.**

26. "Have you read *Oliver Twist* by Dickens?" asked Colleen.

27. "No," said Martina, "but I would like to read it."

28. "Will you tell me about it?" she asked.

29. "Oliver," said Colleen, "was a poor orphan boy."

30. She continued, "He became involved with criminals in London."

F. **Add quotation marks or underlining where needed.**

31. Charles Dickens also wrote the novel Great Expectations.

32. My mother loves that book and a play called The Frozen Deep in which Dickens acted.

33. She also appreciates great art, such as Van Gogh's The Potato Eaters.

34. "Death Be Not Proud" is her favorite poem.

35. She wrote her short story "Awaken" based on it.

Try It Yourself
Write four sentences about one of your favorite books.
Be sure to use capital letters and punctuation marks correctly.

_____

_____

_____

_____

Check Your Own Work
Choose a selection from your writing portfolio, your journal, a work in progress, an assignment from another class, or a letter. Revise it, applying the skills you have reviewed. This checklist will help you.

✔ Do your sentences end with the right punctuation marks?

✔ Have you followed the rules for commas?

✔ Have you used apostrophes and quotation marks correctly?

✔ Have you capitalized all proper nouns and proper adjectives?

Punctuation and Capitalization

Name _____

129. Subjects, Predicates, Direct Objects, Modifiers

A **diagram** shows how the words in a sentence fit together. It highlights the most important words in a sentence and shows how the other words relate to them.

SENTENCE: **The hungry children quickly ate the green grapes.**

Start the diagram by drawing a horizontal line. Find the verb in the sentence and write it in the middle of the line. Find the simple subject and write it in front of the verb. Draw a vertical line between the subject and the verb. The vertical line should cut through the horizontal line.

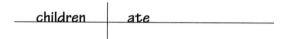

Now find the direct object in the sentence. Write the direct object on the horizontal line to the right of the verb. Draw a vertical line between the verb and the direct object. This line touches the horizontal line but does not cut through it.

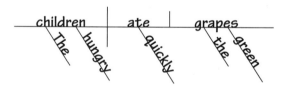

Words that describe the subject, the verb, or the direct object are written on slanting lines under those words.

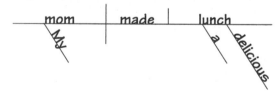

Diagram each of these sentences.

1. My mom made a delicious lunch.

2. The band played my favorite song.

Name _____

3. I carefully planted the tiny seeds.

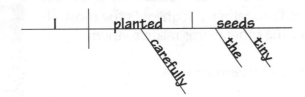

4. The clever girl performed several magic tricks.

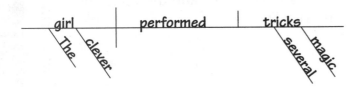

5. The puppy wagged its tail happily.

6. The sleepy children slowly climbed the stairs.

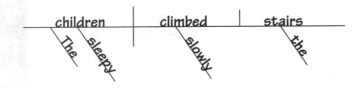

7. Linda's dad quickly fixed her bike.

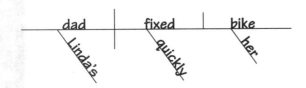

8. The black horse easily jumped the low fence.

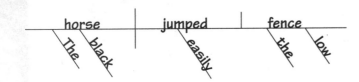

Diagramming

130. Indirect Objects

In a diagram an indirect object is placed on a horizontal line beneath the verb. It is connected to the verb by a slanted line. Words that describe the indirect object go on slanting lines under the indirect object.

SENTENCE: **The teacher gave the students their grades.**

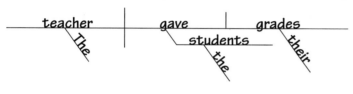

Diagram each of these sentences.

1. Henry's mom made the boys some lemonade.

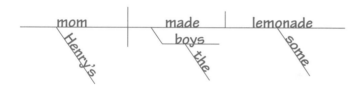

2. The same reporter asked the mayor a question.

3. The babysitter read the sleepy children a story.

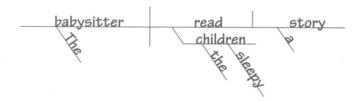

4. My cousin sold me his old telescope.

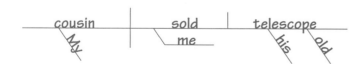

CONTINUED

Diagramming

5. I happily showed my mother my latest painting.

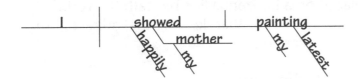

6. Tom is writing his older brother an e-mail.

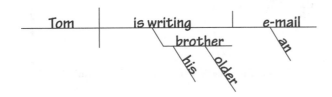

7. The coach handed the players their new uniforms.

8. The ringmaster offered the elephant a peanut.

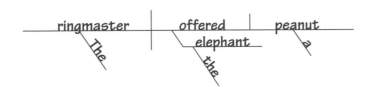

9. My little sister owes me five dollars.

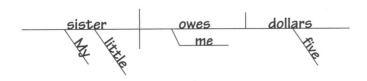

10. The waiter handed each hungry diner a menu.

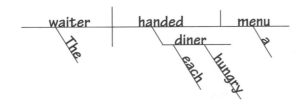

Name _____

131. Subject Complements

In a diagram a subject complement is written on the main horizontal line after the verb. A line that slants back toward the subject separates the subject complement and the verb. The slanting line touches the horizontal line but does not cut through it.

SENTENCE: **That tall man is the basketball coach.**

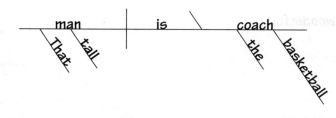

Diagram each of these sentences.

1. Crisp, juicy apples are my favorite fruit.

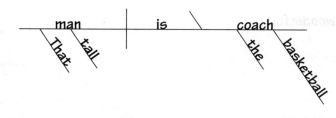

2. The skater's tricks were difficult.

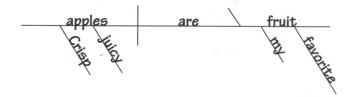

3. The short blond boy is the fastest runner.

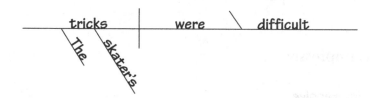

4. My dad is a great cook.

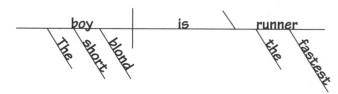

Diagramming

5. Gloria's new skateboard is orange.

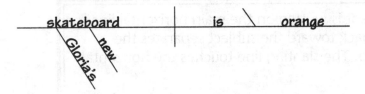

6. That TV show was wonderful.

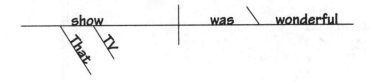

7. George Washington was our first president.

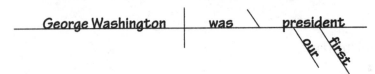

8. Tomorrow could be your lucky day.

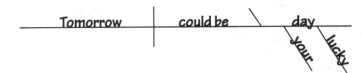

9. Lee Ann's wooden sculpture was impressive.

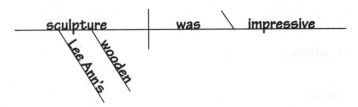

10. The singer's final note was flat.

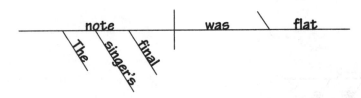

Name _____

132. Prepositional Phrases

In a diagram a prepositional phrase goes beneath the word it describes. The preposition is on a slanting line. The object of the preposition is on a horizontal line that connects to the slanting line. Any word or words that describe the object go on slanting lines under the object.

SENTENCE: **The woman in the red hat gave me a look of total joy.**

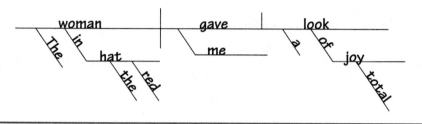

Diagram each of these sentences.

1. The tops of the trees swayed in the wind.

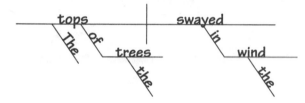

2. My cousin was the winner of the race.

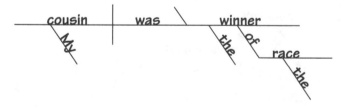

3. Bristlecone pines are the oldest living things on earth.

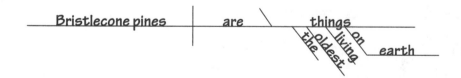

4. The boy on the green bike told his friends a story about a pirate.

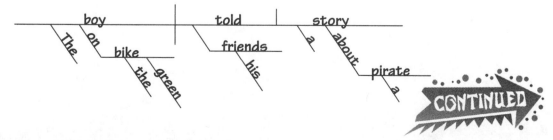

CONTINUED

Name _____

5. The members of the orchestra played several pieces by Mozart.

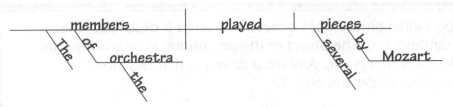

6. Abraham Lincoln was president during the Civil War.

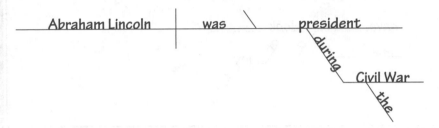

7. After dinner I walked to my friend's house.

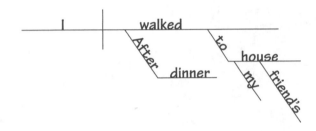

8. The aliens in the movie frightened the children in the audience.

9. The driver gave the reporter from the newspaper a full account of the accident.

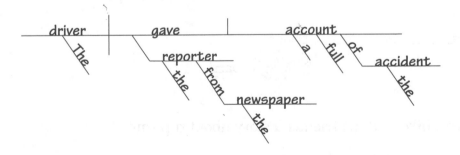

133. Interjections

In a diagram an interjection is placed on a line that is separate from the rest of the sentence. The line is above, at the left of, and parallel to the main horizontal line.

SENTENCE: **Help! The dog is eating my homework.**

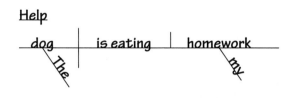

Diagram each of these sentences.

1. Oh, no! Your sister fell into that muddy puddle.

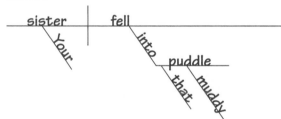

2. Yikes! I almost forgot Mario's birthday!

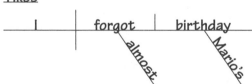

3. Yuck! Who made this pickle smoothie?

4. Oh! The flowers in your garden are beautiful.

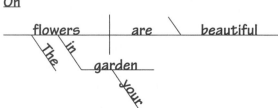

Diagramming

5. Our team won the pennant! Hooray!

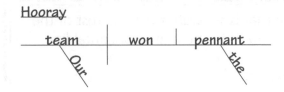

6. Sh! The puppies are sleeping in their basket.

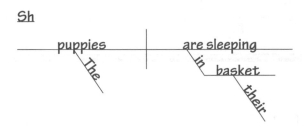

7. Uh-oh! I saw a skunk in the backyard.

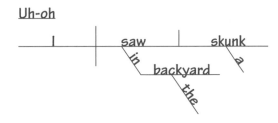

8. Wow! My sister won first prize in the science fair!

9. Ouch! I poked my finger with the needle!

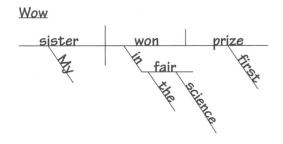

Name _____

134. Compound Subjects and Compound Predicates

In a diagram each part of a compound subject or a compound verb is placed on a separate horizontal line. The coordinating conjunction is placed on a dashed line between the two horizontal lines. The lines are connected to the main horizontal line in the usual position of a subject or a verb.

SENTENCE: **Aaron and Melinda washed and dried the dishes.**

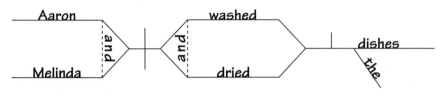

Diagram each of these sentences.

1. The players and the coach celebrated the victory.

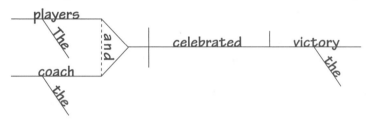

2. Mom steamed zucchini and made fish tacos.

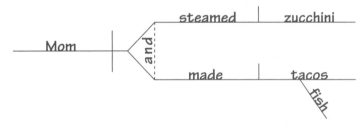

3. Sequoias and redwoods are interesting trees.

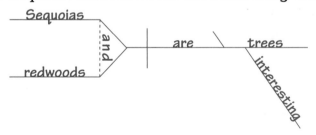

4. Lions and tigers live on separate continents.

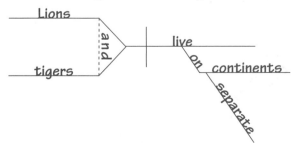

Name _____

5. The children collected cans and took them to the recycling center.

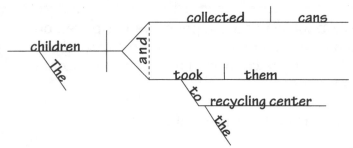

6. Mark and Melissa fed the dog and watered the plants.

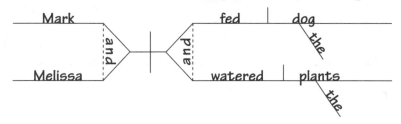

7. Jenny washed and styled her sister's hair.

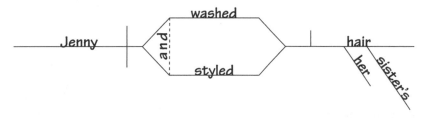

8. A bluebird or a sparrow built a nest in the birdhouse.

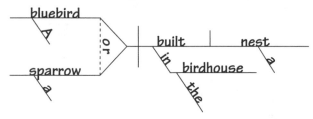

9. Mom gave me a ukulele and taught me a few songs.

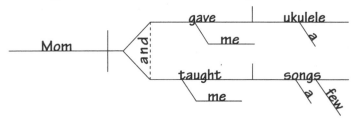

10. Mysteries and science fiction are Carlo's favorite kinds of books.

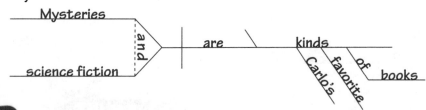

Diagramming

148

135. Compound Direct Objects and Indirect Objects

In a diagram each part of a compound object is placed on a separate horizontal line. The coordinating conjunction is placed on a dashed line between the two horizontal lines. A compound direct object is connected to the main horizontal line and separated from the verb by a vertical line. A compound indirect object is placed under the verb with a slanted line connecting the indirect objects to the main horizontal line.

SENTENCE: **Aunt Clara gave my sister and me lemonade and cookies.**

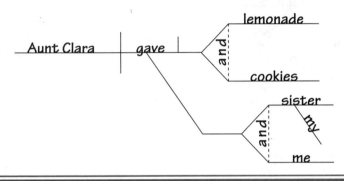

Diagram each of these sentences.

1. Dave took his guitar and his harmonica to the party.

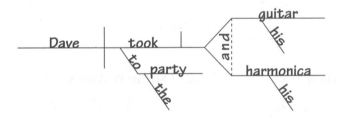

2. The director of the show gave the actors and the musicians their instructions.

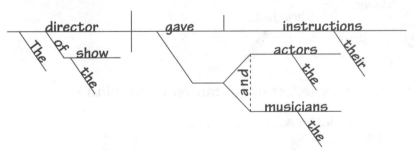

3. Owls often eat mice and other small rodents.

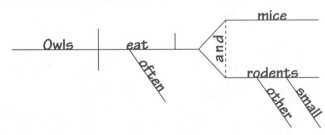

Diagramming

4. The scientist told the interviewer and the audience the results of the experiment.

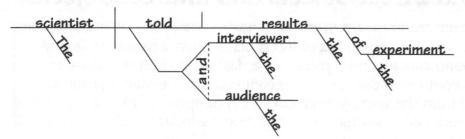

5. The league awarded the winner and the runner-up some trophies and other prizes.

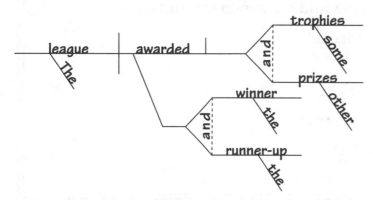

6. The incident taught Kathy and Nate an important lesson about friendship.

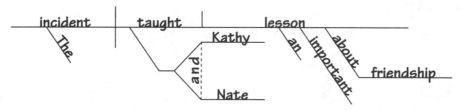

7. The art teacher gave Sandy and Chris a box of paints and some brushes.

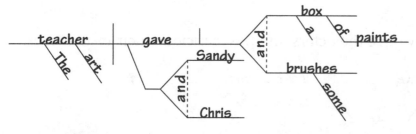

8. We sent the mayor and the governor letters about our recycling plan.

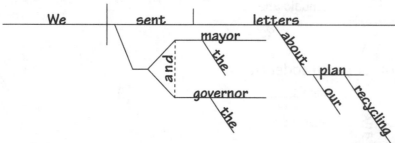

136. Compound Subject Complements

> In a diagram each part of a compound subject complement is placed on a separate horizontal line. The coordinating conjunction is placed on a dashed line between the two horizontal lines. The compound subject complement is connected to the main horizontal line and separated from the verb by a line that slants left.
>
> SENTENCE: **The calm surface of the lake looked cool and inviting.**
>
>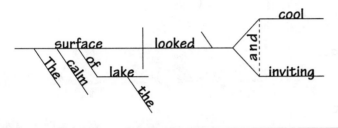

Diagram each of these sentences.

1. The new president of our class will be Connie or Nick.

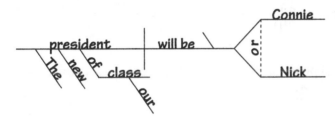

2. The trees around the small pond were tall and shady.

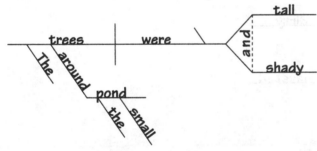

3. My favorite subjects in school are history and math.

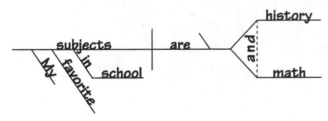

CONTINUED

Diagramming

Name _____

4. The only things in the weedy yard were an old shoe and a bicycle wheel.

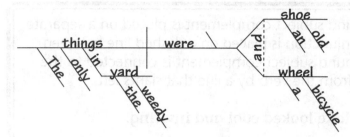

5. A porcupine's quills are sharp and stiff.

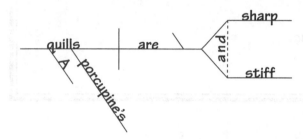

6. The main characters in the story were Pecos Bill and his horse.

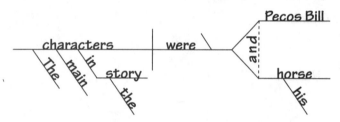

7. After the game the players were dirty and exhausted.

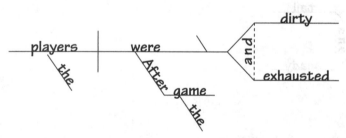

8. Grandma's famous grits are always cheesy and smooth.

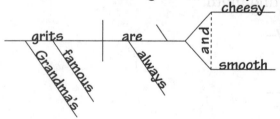

Diagramming

137. Compound Sentences

In a diagram each clause in a compound sentence is placed on its own horizontal line and diagrammed separately. The coordinating conjunction is placed on a dashed vertical line that connects the left edges of the horizontal lines.

SENTENCE: **Chad lost his cell phone, and he hasn't found it anywhere.**

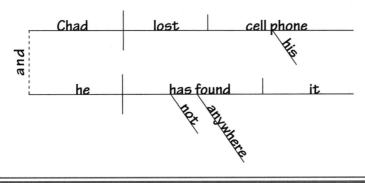

Diagram each of these sentences.

1. The weather was sunny yesterday, but it is cool and rainy today.

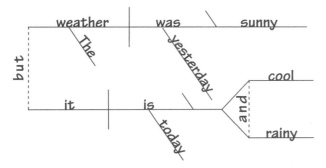

2. I made the sandwiches, and my sister washed the fruit.

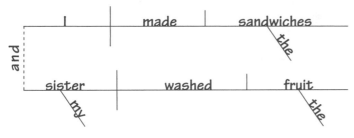

3. The reporter asked the quarterback a question, but he walked away.

4. I might watch TV after dinner, or I might write my friend an e-mail.

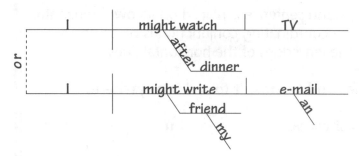

5. Lincoln's speech was short, but everyone remembered it.

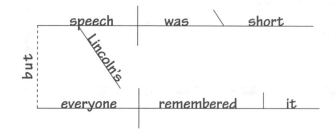

6. The goalie deflected the shot, and our team won the game.

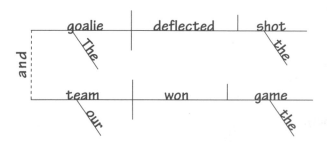

7. My mom offered me a snack, but I wasn't very hungry.

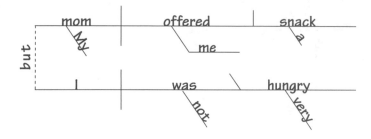

138. Adverb Clauses

In a diagram an adverb clause is placed on a horizontal line under the horizontal line for the independent clause. Each clause is diagrammed separately. The subordinate conjunction is placed on a slanted dashed line that connects the verb in the adverb clause to the word in the independent clause that the adverb clause describes. It usually goes to the verb.

SENTENCE: **As the pioneers crossed the prairie, they faced many hardships.**

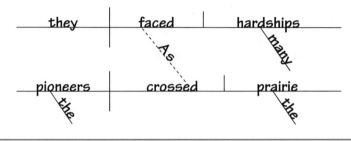

Diagram each of these sentences.

1. When the scientists found the fossils, they called the museum.

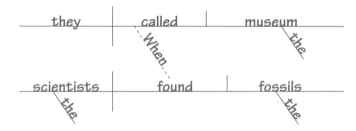

2. I wrote my senator a letter as soon as I heard the news.

3. They will go to the movie after they finish their homework.

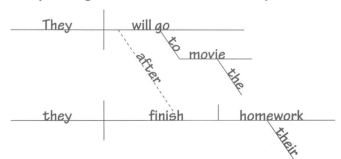

 CONTINUED

4. Before Joe and Nancy grilled the hamburgers, they sliced the tomatoes and the onions.

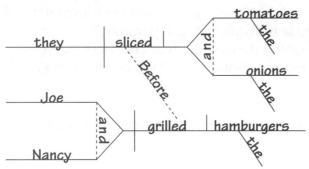

5. Mrs. Chan will work in her flower garden until the sun goes down.

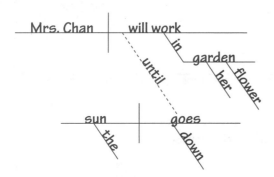

6. The children get excited whenever they see a parade.

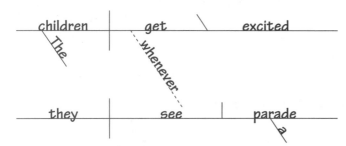

7. We heard the loud crash while we were riding our bikes.

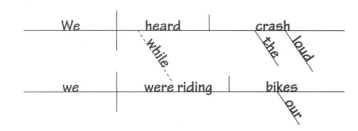

139. Diagramming Review

In a diagram each part of a sentence has its own place.

Diagram each of these sentences.

1. Benjamin Franklin was a scientist and an inventor, and he published a famous almanac.

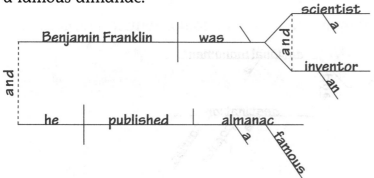

2. After my cousin went to college, my sister and I often sent her cards.

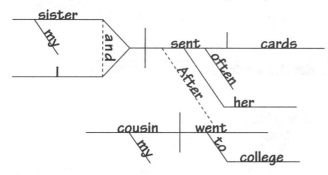

3. *Tyrannosaurus rex* had huge jaws and was a fierce predator.

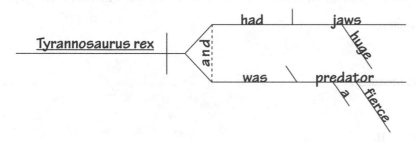

4. My family and I visited Texas in the spring when the wildflowers were blooming.

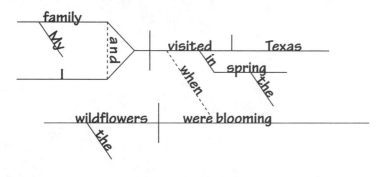

Diagramming

5. Micky is usually the best fielder on the team, but he dropped the fly ball.

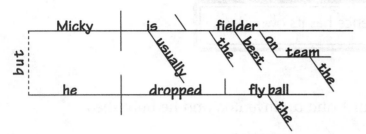

6. Mount Rushmore is a national monument and a popular tourist destination.

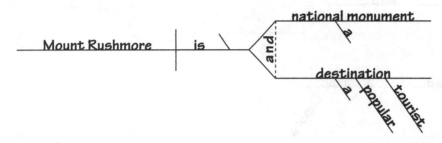

7. Bison are the largest mammals in North America, and some Native Americans raise the giant animals for food.

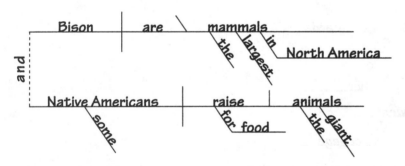

8. The car's engine coughed and sputtered until my dad and my uncle fixed it.

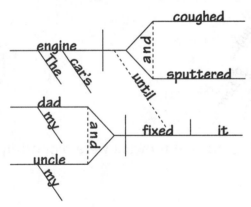

Handbook of Terms

ADJECTIVES

An **adjective** is a word that describes a noun or pronoun.

Articles point out nouns. *A, an,* and *the* are articles.

- *A* and *an* are the indefinite articles. An indefinite article refers to any of a class of things: *a* banana, *an* elephant. *The* is the definite article. The definite article refers to one or more specific things: *A* pear and *an* apple are in *the* blue bowl.

- When two or more nouns joined by *and* name different people, places, or things, use an article before each noun. When two or more nouns joined by *and* refer to the same person, place, or thing, use an article before the first noun only: *The* singer and *the* dancer performed together. *The* actor and comedian is my cousin.

Demonstrative adjectives point out specific persons, places, or things.

- *This* and *that* point out one person, place, or thing.

- *These* and *those* point out more than one person, place, or thing.

- *This* and *these* point out persons, places, or things that are near.

- *That* and *those* point out persons, places, or things that are farther away.

Descriptive adjectives tell about the size, shape, color, weight, or other qualities of the things they describe. A descriptive adjective can come before a noun: *sunny* morning, *hot* day. A descriptive adjective can follow a linking verb: The sun is *warm.*

Interrogative adjectives are used in questions. An interrogative adjective goes before a noun. The interrogative adjectives are *what, which,* and *whose: What* types of books do you enjoy? *Which* book is your favorite? *Whose* book is this?

Possessive adjectives show possession or ownership. A possessive adjective goes before a noun. The possessive adjectives are *my, your* (singular or plural), *his, her, its, our,* and *their: his* skateboard, *their* bikes.

Proper adjectives are adjectives that come from proper nouns. A proper adjective begins with a capital letter: *American* history.

Some adjectives tell exactly how many: *ten, twenty-five, third, twelfth.* Some adjectives tell about how many: *many, few, several, some.*

See also **comparisons, prepositions, sentences.**

ADVERBS

An **adverb** is a word that describes a verb, an adjective, or another adverb.

- An **adverb of time** answers the question *when* or *how often:* It rained *yesterday.* We *usually* eat lunch at noon.

- An **adverb of place** answers the question *where:* Toshi bent his head *forward.* Sit *here* by the gate.

- An **adverb of manner** answers the question *how* or *in what manner:* Jason draws *well.* She dances the waltz *gracefully.*

Like adjectives, some adverbs can be used to compare.

- The **positive degree** of an adverb is the base form: Jonathan skates *quickly.*

- The **comparative degree** compares two actions and is often used with *than:* Jonathan skates *less quickly* than I skate.

- The **superlative degree** compares three or more actions: Jonathan skates *least quickly* of all his relatives.

A negative idea is expressed by using one negative word. That negative word may be *no, not, none, never,* or *nothing.* Those words should be used only in sentences that have no other negative words: I do not have *any* (not *no)* apples.

See also **clauses, comparisons, prepositions.**

ANTECEDENTS

The word to which a pronoun refers is its **antecedent.** The pronoun must agree with its antecedent in person and number. The third person singular must also show whether it refers to a male, a female, or a thing: *Jay* did as *he* was told.

CAPITALIZATION

Many words begin with a capital letter, including the following:

- the first word of a sentence—The bell rang.

- an abbreviation if the word it stands for begins with a capital letter—U.S. government

- titles that precede a person's name—Sir Paul McCartney

- the first word and the name of the person addressed in the salutation of a letter and the first word in the closing of a letter—Dear Marie, Yours truly,

- the first word, the last word, and each important word in the titles of books, plays, works of art, and poems—*A Tale of Two Cities, Romeo and Juliet, Starry Night,* "Fire and Ice"

- the first word of a direct quotation—Mother said, "It's time for my favorite television program."

- proper nouns and proper adjectives—America, American flag

- North, East, South, and West when they refer to a section of the country or the world—the old West. They are not capitalized when they refer to direction—He drove west on Main Street.

- names referring to the deity or to sacred books—God, the Bible

Capital letters are also used for:

- the pronoun *I*

- two-letter state postal abbreviations—MA, NY, CA

- initials in a person's name—I. M. Pei for Ieoh Ming Pei

CLAUSES

A **clause** is a group of words that has a subject and a predicate.

An **adverb clause** is a dependent clause used as an adverb. An adverb clause often answers the question *when:* We ate dinner *before we went to the movie.*

A **dependent clause** does not express a complete thought and cannot stand on its own as a sentence: *before we went to the movie.*

An **independent clause** expresses a complete thought and can stand on its own as a sentence: *We ate dinner.*

COMPARISONS

Many adjectives can be used to compare two or more persons, places, or things.

- An adjective in the **positive degree** describes one or more persons, places, or things: *quiet, powerful, attractive.*

- An adjective in the **comparative degree** compares two persons, places, or things. Form comparative adjectives by adding *-er* to the positive degree or by putting *more* or *less* before the positive degree: *quieter, more powerful, less attractive.*

- An adjective in the **superlative degree** compares three or more persons, places, or things. Form superlative adjectives by adding -*est* to the positive degree or by putting *most* or *least* before the positive degree: *quietest, most powerful, least attractive.*

Fewer and *fewest* refer to number; use them with plural count nouns: There are *fewer* apples than oranges. *Less* and *least* refer to quantity; use them with noncount nouns: My car uses *less* gas than yours.

Some adverbs can be used to compare two or more actions. Those adverbs have positive, comparative, and superlative degrees just as adjectives have.

- Form the comparative degree by adding -*er* to the positive degree or by putting *more* or *less* before the positive degree: *faster, more carefully, less slowly.*

- Form the superlative degree by adding -*est* to the positive degree or by putting *most* or *least* before the positive degree: *fastest, most carefully, least slowly.*

CONJUNCTIONS

A **conjunction** is a word used to connect words or groups of words.

A **coordinating conjunction** connects words or groups of words that are of equal importance. The most common coordinating conjunctions are *and, but,* and *or:* Joshua *and* Leanne cut *and* glued the words *and* the pictures on some posters, *and* Nancy took orders.

A **subordinate conjunction** introduces a dependent clause and connects it to an independent clause. Many subordinate conjunctions tell *when.* They include *after, as, as soon as, before, once, since, when, whenever, while,* and *until:* I'll help you *after* I finish my homework.

CONTRACTIONS

A **contraction** is two words written as one word with one or more letters omitted. An apostrophe (') is used to show the omission of a letter or letters. Subject pronouns are used with some verbs to form contractions: *we're* for *we are, she's* for *she is* or *she has.*

INTERJECTIONS

An **interjection** expresses a strong feeling or emotion. An interjection is followed by an exclamation mark: *Wow! Yikes!*

NOUNS

A **noun** is a name word. It names a person, place, or thing. A noun can be used as the subject, the direct object, the indirect object, the object of a preposition, or the subject complement in a sentence.

A **collective noun** names a group of persons, places, or things that are considered as a unit: The *band* played loudly.

A **common noun** names any one member of a group of persons, places, or things: *queen, city, church*.

Count nouns name items that can be counted separately. A count noun has a singular form and a plural form: *cherries, emotions, chairs*.

A noun is used in **direct address** when it names the person spoken to: *Carol*, would you help me?

Noncount nouns name items that cannot be counted separately. A noncount noun generally takes a verb that agrees with *he, she,* or *it*. A noncount noun does not have a plural form: *fruit, anger, furniture*.

A **plural noun** names more than one person, place, or thing: *boys, rivers, berries*.

A **possessive noun** expresses possession or ownership. The apostrophe (') is the sign of a possessive noun.

- To form the possessive of a singular noun, add *-'s* to the singular form: *architect's*

- To form the possessive of a plural noun that ends in *-s*, add an apostrophe to the plural form: *farmers'*

- To form the possessive of a plural noun that does not end in *-s*, add *-'s* to the plural form: *children's*

A **proper noun** names a particular person, place, or thing. A proper noun is capitalized: *Queen Elizabeth, London, Westminster Abbey*.

A **singular noun** names one person, place, or thing: *boy, river, berry*.

PREPOSITIONS

A **preposition** is a word that shows the relationship between a noun or a pronoun and another word in a sentence. The noun or pronoun that follows the preposition is the **object of the proposition:** The huge mountain lion leaped *through* (preposition) the tall *grass* (object of the preposition).

A **prepositional phrase** is a phrase that is introduced by a preposition.

- An **adjective phrase** is used as an adjective and describes a noun: The cabin *in the woods* burned down.

- An **adverb phrase** is used as an adverb and usually describes a verb: The river flows *into the sea.*

PRONOUNS

A **pronoun** is a word that takes the place of a noun or nouns.

Demonstrative pronouns point out people, places, and things. The singular demonstrative pronouns are *this* and *that.* The plural demonstrative pronouns are *these* and *those. This* and *these* point out things that are near *These* are my marbles here. *That* and *those* point out things that are farther away: *That* is my house over there.

An **intensive pronoun** is used to emphasize the noun that comes before it. The intensive pronouns are *myself, yourself, himself, herself, itself, ourselves, yourselves,* and *themselves:* He *himself* baked the pie.

An **interrogative pronoun** is used to ask a question. The interrogative pronouns are *who, whom, what,* and *whose. Who* is used when the person is the subject of the sentence: *Who* sneezed? *Whom* is used when the person is the object of a verb or a preposition: *Whom* can I thank?

An **object pronoun** may be used as the direct object or the indirect object of a verb or as the object of a preposition. The object pronouns are *me, you* (singular or plural), *him, her, it, us,* and *them:* I saw *her* at the mall. I showed *her* a great T-shirt. She bought it for *him.*

A **personal pronoun** has different forms.

- A personal pronoun shows **person:** the speaker **(first person),** the person spoken to **(second person),** or the person, place, or thing spoken about **(third person).** The first person pronouns are *I, me, mine, we, us,* and *ours.* The second person pronouns are *you* and *yours.* The third person pronouns are *he, him, his, she, her, hers, it, its, they, them,* and *theirs.*

- A personal pronoun shows **number: singular or plural.** A personal pronoun is **singular** when it refers to one person, place, or thing. A personal pronoun is **plural** when it refers to more than one person, place, or thing. The singular pronouns are *I, me, mine, you, yours, she, her, hers, he, him, his, it,* and *its.* The plural pronouns are *we, us, ours, you, yours, they, them,* and *theirs.*

- The third person singular personal pronoun can refer to a male (*he, him, his*), a female (*she, her, hers*), or a thing (*it, its*).

A **possessive pronoun** shows possession or ownership. The possessive pronouns are *mine, yours, his, hers, its, ours,* and *theirs.* Although possessive pronouns show ownership, they do not contain apostrophes: The new skates are *hers.*

A **reflexive pronoun** can be used as a direct object or an indirect object or as the object of a preposition. Reflexive pronouns usually refer to the subject of the sentence. The reflexive pronouns are *myself, yourself, himself, herself, itself, ourselves, yourselves,* and *themselves:* The man helped *himself.* He made *himself* a sandwich. Gwen walked by *herself.*

A **subject pronoun** may be used as the subject or as a subject complement. The subject pronouns are *I, you* (singular or plural), *he, she, it, we,* and *they.*

See also **antecedents.**

PUNCTUATION

An **apostrophe** (') is used as follows:

- to show ownership—the *cook's* hat, the *girls'* horses

- to replace a letter or letters left out in a contraction—*he'll* for *he will, I'm* for *I am*

Commas (,) are used to make reading clearer. Among the many uses of a comma are the following:

- to separate three or more words or groups of words in a series—We saw elephants, giraffes, hyenas, and monkeys.

- to set off parts of dates—January 1, 2009

- to set off parts of addresses—321 Spring Rd., Apt. 4

- to separate a city and a state—Atlanta, GA

- to set off words in direct address—Josie, I'm so pleased that you called me this morning.

- after the word *yes* or *no* when it introduces a sentence—Yes, I agree with you completely.

- to set off direct quotations, except where a question mark or an exclamation point is needed—
    "We have only vanilla and chocolate today," he said in an apologetic tone.
    "Fantastic!" Lena shouted.

- to separate independent clauses connected by the conjunctions *and, but,* and *or*—She called his name, but he didn't answer her.

- after the salutation in a friendly letter and the closing in all letters—Dear Ben, Sincerely yours,

An **exclamation point** (!) is used after an interjection or an exclamatory sentence: Wonderful! What a celebration that was!

A **period** (.) is used at the end of a declarative sentence or an imperative sentence and after initials and some abbreviations: Dr. H. L. Martin is here. Please invite him to sit down.

A **question mark** (?) is used at the end of a question: What time is it?

Quotation marks (" ") are used as follows:

- before and after every direct quotation and every part of a divided quotation—
  "Let's go shopping," said Michiko.
  "I can go with you," Father said, "after I have eaten lunch."

- to enclose titles of short stories, poems, songs, and magazine articles. Titles of magazines, newspapers, movies, plays, TV shows, works of art, and most books are usually printed in *italics* or are underlined—I read "A Tribute to Heroes" in *Time for Kids*.

SENTENCES

A **sentence** is a group of words that expresses a complete thought.

A **complex sentence** contains one independent clause and one dependent clause: After Frida caught a cold, she went to bed.

A **compound sentence** contains two or more independent clauses. An independent clause has a subject and a predicate, and it can stand alone as a sentence. A compound sentence is formed by connecting two independent clauses with a comma and the coordinating conjunction *and, but,* or *or.* A semicolon may be used instead of the comma and conjunction: We went to the park, *and* we played softball. It started to rain; we ran home.

A **declarative sentence** makes a statement. It ends with a period: The sun is shining.

An **exclamatory sentence** expresses strong or sudden emotion. It ends with an exclamation point: What a loud noise that was!

An **imperative sentence** gives a command or makes a request. It usually ends with a period: Go to the store. Please pick up the papers.

An **interrogative sentence** asks a question. It ends with a question mark: Where is my pen?

A sentence is made up of a subject and a predicate.

- The **subject** names the person, place, or thing a sentence is about. The **simple subject** is a noun or pronoun: The tall young *man* is riding. The **complete subject** is the simple subject with all the words that describe it: *The tall young man* is riding.

- The **predicate** tells something about the subject. The **simple predicate** is a verb or verb phrase: Teresa *waved* to the child. The **complete predicate** is the verb with all its objects, complements, and describing words: Teresa *waved to the child*.

- The **direct object** answers the question *whom* or *what* after an action verb in a sentence: Nathaniel fed the *baby*. An object pronoun can be used as a direct object: Nathaniel fed *him*.

- The **indirect object** tells to whom, for whom, to what, or for what an action is done. The indirect object comes between the verb and the direct object: Kim gave *Laura* a present.

- The **subject complement** is a word that completes the meaning of a linking verb in a sentence. A subject complement may be a noun, a pronoun, or an adjective: Broccoli is a green *vegetable*. The winner was *she*. The sea will be *cold*.

Sentence order is the sequence of the subject and verb in a sentence.

- When the verb in a sentence follows the subject, the sentence is in **natural order**: The *settlers planted* the seeds.

- When the main verb or the helping verb in a sentence comes before the subject, the sentence is in **inverted order**: Across the plain *marched* the tired *soldiers*.

If a sentence has two or more simple subjects, it has a **compound subject:** *Ivan* and *John* argued with the grocer.

If a sentence has two or more predicates, it has a **compound predicate:** The toddler *walks* and *plays* well.

If a sentence has two or more direct objects, it has a **compound direct object:** Wear your *hat, scarf,* and *gloves*.

If a sentence has two or more subject complements, it has a **compound subject complement:** The winners were *Steve* and *Patty*.

SUBJECT–VERB AGREEMENT

A subject and a verb must agree.

- Singular nouns, including noncount nouns, and third person singular pronouns (*he, she,* and *it*) take verbs that end in *-s* or *-es* in the simple present tense: Kendra *makes* maps. Laughter *makes* a nice sound.

- Plural nouns, plural pronouns, and the singular pronouns *I* and *you* must have verbs that do not end in *-s* or *-es*: We *run.* Cattle *run.*

- Use *am* or *was* with the first person singular pronoun: I *am* a soccer player. I *was* late for practice.

- Use *is* or *was* with a singular noun or a third person singular pronoun: Paris *is* a city. Fruit *is* nutritious. She *was* a pianist.

- Use *are* or *were* with a plural noun, the second person subject pronoun, or the third person plural pronoun: Dogs *are* good pets. You *are* the winner. We *were* happy. They *were* my neighbors.

- Use *doesn't* with a singular noun or a singular third person pronoun: He *doesn't* have a pencil. The furniture *doesn't* cost much. She *doesn't* have a pen.

- Use *don't* with a plural noun, a first person pronoun, a second person pronoun, or a third person plural pronoun: Buses *don't* stop here. We *don't* have to go. You *don't* have the tickets.

TENSE

The tense of a verb shows the time of its action.

- The **simple present tense** tells about something that is always true or about an action that happens again and again. I *play* the piano every afternoon.

- The **simple past tense** tells about an action that happened in the past. The past tense of regular verbs ends in *-ed:* Lucia *raced* to the end of the block.

- The **future tense** tells about an action that will happen in the future. The future tense can be formed with *will* and the present part of the verb: They *will come* to the game on Sunday. The future tense can also be made from a form of the verb *be* with *going to* and the present part of the verb: I *am going to play* shortstop.

- The **present progressive tense** tells what is happening now. The present progressive tense is formed with a present form of *be* and the present participle: He *is eating* his lunch now.

- The **past progressive tense** tells what was happening in the past. The past progressive tense is formed with a past form of *be* and the present participle: We *were snoring* loudly last night.

- The **future progressive tense** tells what will be happening in the future; the future progressive is formed with *will, be, am going to be, is going to be,* or *are going to be* and the present participle: They *are going to be celebrating* their birthdays next week. He *will be going* South.

- The **present perfect tense** tells about an action that happened at some indefinite time in the past or an action that started in the past and continues into the present time. The present perfect tense is formed with *has* or *have* and the past participle: We *have lived* here for two years.

- The **past perfect tense** tells about a past action that was completed before another action in the past. The past perfect tense is formed with *had* and the past participle: She *had finished* her homework by 6 o'clock.

- The **future perfect tense** tells about a future event that will be started and completed before another future event. The future perfect tense is formed with *will have* and the past participle: We *will have eaten* lunch by the time you get here.

VERBS

A **verb** is a word that expresses action or being.

A **linking verb** links a subject with a subject complement (a noun, a pronoun, or an adjective). Verbs of being are linking verbs: She *is* a teacher. The winner *was* he. The children *will be* happy.

A verb has four **principal parts:** the **present,** the **present participle,** the **past,** and the **past participle.**

- The present participle is formed by adding *-ing* to the present: jumping, singing. For verbs that end in *e,* drop the final *e* and add *-ing:* drive, driving. For verbs that end in a consonant following a vowel, double the consonant before adding *-ing:* stop, stopping. The present participle is often used with a form of the helping verb *be* (*am, is, are, was, were* or *been*).

- The past and the past participle of regular verbs are formed by adding *-d* or *-ed* to the present: bake, baked, jump, jumped. For verbs that end in a consonant following a vowel, form the past participle by doubling the consonant before adding *-ing:* hum, hummed. The past participle is often used with the helping verb *have, has,* or *had.*

- The simple past and the past participle of irregular verbs are not formed by adding *-ed* to the present: sang, sung.

A **verb phrase** is a group of words that does the work of a single verb. A verb phrase contains one or more helping verbs (such as *is, are, has, have, will, can, could, would, should*) and a main verb: She *had tripped* over the rug twice before I saw her.